Eighteen

THE
FLORIDA
NOTARY LAW
PRIMER

*All the hard-to-find information
every Florida Notary Public
needs to know!*

National Notary Association

Published by

National Notary Association
9350 De Soto Ave.
Chatsworth, CA 91311-4926
(818) 739-4000
Fax: (818) 700-0920
Website: www.NationalNotary.org
Email: nna@NationalNotary.org

The information in this *Primer* is correct and current at the time
of its publication, although new laws, regulations and rulings may
subsequently affect the validity of certain sections. This information
is provided to aid comprehension of state Notary Public requirements
and should not be construed as legal advice. Please consult an
attorney for inquires relating to legal matters.

Eighteenth Edition, Sixth Printing
First Edition © 1982

ISBN: 978-1-59767-071-5
L.C. Control Number: 2005920443

Table
of Contents

Introduction 1

How to Become a Florida Notary 3

Tools of the Trade. 5

10 Most-Asked Questions. 7

Steps to Proper Notarization. 12

Notary Laws Explained 16
    The Notary Commission 16
    Official Notarial Acts. 21
    Practices and Procedures. 38
    Misconduct, Fines and Penalties 64
    Electronic Notarization 68

Test Your Knowledge 75

Florida Laws Pertaining to Notaries Public 81

Sample Ceremony in Spanish/
    Ejemplo de Ceremonia en Español 116

Offices of Florida Notary Regulating Officials 117

Bureaus of Vital Statistics. 118

Hague Convention Nations 122

About the NNA 125

Index 127

For the latest updates on state laws
and requirements, please visit

www.NationalNotary.org/Primer-Updates

Have a Tough Notary Question?

If you were an NNA member, you could get the answer to that
difficult question. Join the NNA and your membership includes
access to the Notary Hotline* and live Notary experts providing the
latest Notary information regarding laws, rules and regulations.

Hours

Monday – Friday	5:00 a.m. – 7:00 p.m. (PT)
Saturdays	5:00 a.m. – 5:00 p.m. (PT)

Hotline Toll-Free Phone Number: 1-888-876-0827

After hours you can leave a message or email our experts at
Hotline@NationalNotary.org and they will respond the next business day.

*Access to the Notary Hotline is for NNA members only. Call and become a
member today.

Introduction

You are to be commended on your interest in Florida Notary law! Purchasing *The Florida Notary Law Primer* identifies you as a conscientious professional who takes your official duties seriously.

In few fields is the expression "more to it than meets the eye" truer than in Notary law. What often appears on the surface to be a simple procedure may, in fact, have important legal considerations.

The purpose of *The Florida Notary Law Primer* is to provide you with a resource to help decipher the many intricate laws that affect notarization. In so doing, the *Primer* will acquaint you with all of the important aspects of Florida's Notary laws and with prudent notarial practices in general.

The Florida Notary Law Primer has been periodically revised and updated since its initial publication in 1982. This edition of the Primer contains the 2008 legislative changes to the Florida Statutes enacting the Uniform Real Property Electronic Recording Act (URPERA) which enables county recorders to accept electronic documents in land records as well as the 2010 Administrative Rules affecting electronic notarization.

While *The Florida Notary Law Primer* begins with informative chapters on how to obtain your commission, what tools the Notary needs, often-asked questions and critical steps in notarization, the heart of this book is the chapter entitled "Notary Laws Explained." Here, we take you through the myriad of Notary laws and put them in easy-to-understand terms. Every section of the law is analyzed and explained, as well as topics not covered by Florida law but nonetheless of vital concern to you as a Notary.

For handy reference, we have reprinted the complete text of the laws of Florida that relate to Notaries Public. In addition, we have included addresses and phone numbers of pertinent offices of the Department of State, the Governor and Bureaus of Vital Statistics, plus a list of nations that are parties to the Hague Convention, a treaty simplifying the process of authentication.

Whether you're about to be commissioned for the first time or a longtime Notary, we're sure that *The Florida Notary Law Primer* will provide you with new insight and understanding.

> Milton G. Valera
> Chairman
> National Notary Association

How to Become a Florida Notary

1. Ensure that you comply with the basic qualifications for a Florida Notary commission.[1]

First, you must be at least 18 years of age; and second, you must be a legal resident of the state. U.S. citizenship is not required as long as you legally reside in this country under federal law. If you are a permanent resident, you must file a recorded Declaration of Domicile with your application.

2. Obtain a commission application.

The official application for a Florida Notary commission may be obtained by writing or calling:

> Department of State
> Division of Corporations
> Notary Commissions
> P.O. Box 6800
> Tallahassee, FL 32314
> (850) 245-6975

Included with the Notary application will be a blank Notary bond form.[2]

If you are renewing your current Notary commission, you must go through the same process as if applying for a new commission — though you need not take the three-hour course described on page 4.

---

1. IMPORTANT NOTE: Laws have created the position of "Civil-law Notary," for which Florida attorneys who have practiced law for five years may qualify — see page 89. Florida Civil-Law Notaries have all of the powers of a regular Florida Notary, but may additionally perform "authentic acts" under civil law for use in foreign nations.

2. In many cases, bonding companies will provide the application forms and submit the completed application package for the Notary applicant. The completeness and timely submission of the package, however, is still the applicant's responsibility.

3. Complete a course on notarization.

Within one year before applying, every first-time applicant must take and pass an interactive or classroom course on Notary duties (including electronic notarization) of at least three hours, from a private or public agency approved by the Governor's office.[3] A certificate proving course completion must then be submitted with the application or be given to the bonding firm handling the application.

4. Complete the application with affidavit.

Using the exact name that you wish to appear on your commission and seal, complete the application in ink, printing neatly or typing. You may not use a fictitious or assumed name.

Included on the application is an affidavit testifying to your good character that must be filled-out and signed by a nonrelative who has known you for one year or more.

5. Purchase your bond.

To protect the public from your intentional or unintentional misconduct as a Notary, you must purchase a bond. Notaries must obtain a $7,500 bond that guarantees up to $7,500 will be paid to any person financially damaged as a result of a Notary's misconduct.

6. Submit the application package.

Forward the following to the Secretary of State: the $39 fee (check or money order, payable to the Florida Department of State); the completed application, including the oath of office and affidavit of good character; a certificate proving course completion; the Notary bond form, completed by the surety company; and, if you are a permanent resident, a recorded Declaration of Domicile.

7. Purchase your seal.

Upon receiving the commissioning document from the Department of State, you must purchase a Notary seal and, on the starting date of your appointment, you may begin performing notarial acts. Safeguard your commission paper, your seal and your official records. ■

---

3. Approved online interactive Notary courses are offered by the State of Florida (*www.dos.state.fl.us*) and the National Notary Association (*www.NationalNotary.org*).

Tools of the Trade

There are several tools that Notaries need to carry out their duties lawfully and efficiently. These tools are as important to the Notary as a hammer and saw are to the carpenter.

Inking Seal

The inking seal is the Notary's official seal of office for paper documents. Its impression reproduces photographically, a legal requirement. The seal — affixed using black ink — must include the Notary's name, the words "Notary Public — State of Florida" and the Notary's commission number and expiration date.

Seal Embosser

While not required by Florida law, the seal embosser is used in many states and is often expected on documents sent abroad. Many Florida Notaries opt to affix an embossment in addition to the legally required inked-seal impression. The seal embosser makes a non-photographically reproducible indentation on the document. Because photocopies of documents can sometimes easily pass as originals today, the embossment can be used to distinguish an original from a photocopy. Also, embossing all pages in a document together can safeguard against the substitution or addition of pages.

Journal of Notarial Acts

Though Florida law does not require Notaries to keep a record of their official acts, the Governor's office encourages such recordkeeping by every Notary.

The Notary's journal provides a record of notarizations that may be used as evidence in a court proceeding, and it may protect a Notary against claims of misconduct or negligence.

Information recorded in the journal should include the date, time and type of each official act; the type of document notarized; the signature and printed name of signer; the type of information used to identify the signer; the fee charged, if any; and any additional comments the Notary considers important.

Bound Notary journals with numbered pages have proven to be the safest and most fraud-resistant type of record book. By contrast, loose-leaf books are the least secure.

Jurat Stamp

The jurat stamp impresses on an affidavit the jurat wording "Subscribed and sworn to before me this _____ day of _____, _____ by _____, ..." The jurat stamp is more convenient (and safer, since critical wording will not be omitted) than typing the wording on each affidavit that requires it.

Venue Stamp

The venue stamp imprints the phrase, "State of _____, County of _____," that indicates where the notarization was executed. This stamp is also usable in conjunction with the jurat stamp.

Fingerprinting Device

Though not required by law, asking a signer to leave a thumbprint in the Notary's journal is a strong deterrent to fraud. Small, inexpensive devices make taking a print easy.

Notarial Certificates

Preprinted notarial certificates for acknowledgments, jurats and copy certifications are available.

Errors and Omissions Insurance

Notary errors and omissions insurance provides protection for Notaries who are sued for damages resulting from unintentional notarial mistakes. In the event of a lawsuit, the "E&O" insurance company will provide and pay for the Notary's legal counsel and absorb any damages levied by a court or agreed to in a settlement, up to the policy limit. Errors and omissions insurance does not cover the Notary for intentional misconduct. ■

As a full-service organization, the National Notary Association makes available to Florida Notaries all notarial items required by law, custom and convenience.

10 Most-Asked Questions

Every Notary has a question or two about whether and how to notarize. But there are certain questions that pop up again and again. These top 10 are asked repeatedly at the National Notary Association's seminars, its annual Conference of Notaries Public, and through its Notary Information Service.

As with most questions about notarization, the answer is not always a simple "yes" or "no." Rather, the answer sometimes is "It depends."

Here's what every Notary wants to know:

1. Can I notarize a will?

It depends. A Notary should only notarize a document described as a will if clear instructions and a notarial certificate are provided. If the signer of the will is relying upon the Notary for advice on how to proceed, the Notary should tell the individual to see an attorney.

Laws regarding wills differ from state to state. Some states do not require the notarization of wills, while others allow it as one of several witnessing options. Usually, it is not the will itself that is notarized, but accompanying affidavits signed by witnesses.

The danger in notarizing wills is that would-be testators who have drafted their own wills without legal advice may believe that notarization will make their wills legal and valid. However, even when notarized, such homemade wills may be worthless because the testators failed to obtain the proper number of witnesses, or they omitted important information.

In fact, notarization itself may actually void an otherwise properly executed handwritten (holographic) will, because courts have occasionally held that any writing on the document other than the testator's invalidates the will.

2. Can I notarize for a stranger with no identification?

Yes. If the identification of a signer cannot be based upon personal knowledge or identification documents (ID cards), a Notary may rely upon the oath or affirmation of one personally known credible identifying witness or two credible identifying witnesses who are strangers to the Notary but have acceptable identification themselves, to identify an unknown signer.

If one credible identifying witness is used, the Notary must personally know the credible identifying witness, who must personally know the document signer. This establishes a chain of personal knowledge from the Notary to the credible identifying witness to the signer.

If two credible identifying witnesses are used, both must have proper identification, such as a driver's license, official non-driver's ID or a passport.

A credible identifying witness should be someone the Notary believes to be trustworthy and impartial. If a person has a financial or other beneficial interest in a document, that individual could not act as a reliable witness. To ensure truthfulness, the Notary must obtain a sworn, written statement from each credible identifying witness.

When no credible identifying witness is available to identify a stranger without IDs, the Notary may have no choice but to tell the signer to find a personally known Notary or a friend who personally knows a Notary.

3. Can I notarize a photograph?

No. To simply stamp and sign a photograph is improper. A Notary's signature and seal must only appear on a notarial certificate (such as an acknowledgment or jurat) accompanying a written statement signed by another person.

However, a signature on a written statement referring to an accompanying or attached photograph may be notarized; if the photograph is large enough, the statement and notarial certificate might even appear on its reverse side. Such a format may be acceptable when notarized photos are requested by persons seeking medical or health licenses, or by legal residents renewing foreign passports.

A word of caution here: a Notary should always be suspicious about notarizing a photo-bearing card or document that could be used as a bogus "official" ID.

4. What if there's no room for my seal or if it smears?

Usually, if notarial wording printed on a document leaves no room for a seal, a loose certificate can be attached and filled out instead, if the certificate wording is substantially the same as on the document.

If an initial seal impression is unreadable and there is ample room on the document, another impression may be affixed nearby. The illegibility of the first impression will indicate why a second seal impression was necessary. The Notary should then record in the journal (if kept) that a second seal was applied.

A Notary should never attempt to fix an imperfect seal impression with pen, ink or correction fluid. This may be viewed as evidence of tampering and cause the document's rejection by a receiving agency.

5. Can I notarize signatures on faxes or photocopies of documents?

Yes. A photocopy may be notarized as long as it bears an original signature, meaning that the photocopy must have been signed with pen and ink. A photocopied signature may never be notarized.

Similarly, a faxed document must be signed in ink. In addition, if a faxed document is on thermal paper (the slick paper used in older fax machines), the document should be photocopied onto regular copy paper to avoid the fading of any printed matter and to allow the affixation of signatures and the Notary's seal.

Note that some public recorders may not accept notarized signatures on photocopied documents because they will not adequately reproduce in microfilming.

When carbon copies are made, the Notary will sometimes be asked to conform rather than to notarize the copies. To conform a copy, the Notary reaffixes the official seal on the copy (carbon will not readily transfer a seal impression) and writes "Conformed Copy" prominently across the copy.

6. May I notarize for customers only?

It depends. As a public official, a Notary is not commissioned to serve just the customers or clients of any one business, even when the employer has paid for the bond, commissioning fees and notarial supplies. There is no such officer as a "Notary Private."

It is ethically improper — although hardly ever explicitly prohibited by statute — to discriminate between customers and noncustomers in offering or refusing to offer notarial services and in charging or not charging fees.

Discrimination against anyone who presents a lawful request for notarization is not a suitable policy for a public official commissioned to serve all of the public equally. Also, such discrimination can provide the basis for lawsuits.

However, the *Governor's Reference Manual* has established a provision whereby a Notary and employer may agree to limit his or her services to transactions directly related to the employer's business during business hours. This does not permit discrimination between customers and noncustomers, but only between business-related and nonbusiness-related documents.

7. Can I notarize a document in a language I can't read?

Yes. As long as the notarial certificate and document signature are in a language the Notary can read, Florida Notaries may notarize documents written in languages they cannot read.

However, there are certain difficulties and dangers in notarizing documents that the Notary cannot read. The main difficulty for the Notary is making an accurate journal description of an unreadable document. The main danger to the public and the Notary is that the document may be blatantly fraudulent.

If the signer does not speak English, the document must be in a language that the signer does understand before the notarization may take place. Under no circumstances should a notarization be performed if the Notary and the principal signer cannot communicate in the same language.

8. Can I certify a copy of a birth certificate?

No. Copies of documents that are either vital records or public records should never be certified by Notaries. Only an officer in a Bureau of Vital Statistics should certify a copy of a birth certificate or other vital public record. A Notary's "certification" of a birth or death record may actually lend credibility to a counterfeit or tampered document. Only a county recording official should certify a copy of a deed or other recordable document.

In states such as Florida that allow Notary-certified copies, the types of documents of which Notaries may properly certify copies are original personal papers, such as college diplomas, letters and in-house business documents.

9. Does a document have to be signed in my presence?

No and yes. Documents requiring acknowledgments do not need to be signed in the Notary's presence. However, the signer must appear before the Notary at the time of notarization to acknowledge that he or she freely signed for the purposes stated in the document.

An acknowledgment certificate indicates that the signer personally appeared before the Notary, was identified by the Notary and acknowledged to the Notary that the document was signed without coercion.

On the other hand, documents requiring a jurat must be signed in the Notary's presence, as dictated by the typical jurat wording, "Subscribed (signed) and sworn to before me ...."

A jurat certificate indicates that the signer personally appeared before the Notary, was identified by the Notary, signed in the Notary's presence and was given an oath or affirmation by the Notary.

10. Can I notarize for a family member?

No and yes. State law specifically prohibits Notaries from notarizing for spouses, sons, daughters, mothers or fathers. There is no law, however, that prohibits notarizing for brothers, sisters, cousins and so on. When considering possible notarizations for relatives, the Notary should always consider whether he or she has any personal beneficial interest in the transaction.

Besides the possibility of a financial interest in notarizing for a relative, there may be an "emotional interest" that can prevent the Notary from acting impartially. For example, a Notary who is asked to notarize a contract signed by his or her brother might attempt to persuade the sibling to sign or not sign. As a sibling, the individual is entitled to exert influence — but this is entirely improper for a Notary.

Even if a Notary has no direct beneficial interest in the document and does not attempt to influence the signer, notarizing for a relative could subject the document to a legal challenge if other parties to the transaction allege that the Notary could not have acted impartially. ■

Steps to Proper Notarization

If a Notary can convincingly show that he or she used every reasonable precaution expected of a person of ordinary prudence and intelligence, then the Notary has exercised reasonable care — a shield against liability.

What constitutes reasonable care?

The following 14-step checklist will help Notaries apply reasonable care and avoid the most common pitfalls.

1. Require every signer to personally appear.

The signer must appear in person before the Notary on the date and in the county stated in the notarial certificate. "Personal appearance" means that the signer is in the Notary's physical presence — face to face in the same room. A telephone call is not acceptable as personal appearance.

2. Make a careful identification.

The Notary should identify every document signer through either personal knowledge, the oath of one or two credible identifying witnesses or reliable ID cards.

When using ID cards, the Notary must examine them closely to detect alteration, counterfeiting or evidence that they have been issued to an impostor. Do not rely upon a type of card with which you are unfamiliar, unless you check it against a reference such as the *U.S. Identification Manual* or the *ID Checking Guide*.

3. Feel certain the signer understands the document.

A conscientious and careful Notary will be certain not only of the signer's identity and willingness to sign, but also will make a layperson's judgment about the signer's ability to understand the document, as required by Florida law. In addition, Florida Notaries may not notarize a document if he or she knows that the signer has been judged mentally incapacitated.

A document signer who cannot respond intelligibly in a simple conversation with the Notary should not be considered able to sign at that moment. If in doubt, the Notary can ask the signer if he or she understands the document and can explain its purpose. Or, if in a medical environment, the signer's doctor can be consulted.

4. Check the signature.

The Notary must make sure that the document signer signs the same name appearing on the identification presented.

To check for possible forgery, the Notary should compare the signature that the person leaves in any journal of notarial acts against the signatures on the document and on the IDs. Also, it should be noted whether the signer appears to be laboring on the journal signature, a possible indication of forgery in progress.

Generally, an abbreviated form of a name (John D. Smith instead of John David Smith, for example), is acceptable. However, deviation is only allowed if the individual is signing with less than and not more than what is on the identification document.

5. Look for blank spaces.

Florida Notaries are expressly prohibited by law from notarizing incomplete documents.

Documents with blank spaces have a great potential for fraudulent misuse. A borrower, for example, might sign an incomplete promissory note, trusting the lender to fill it out, only to discover later that the lender has written in an amount in excess of what was actually borrowed.

If the blanks are inapplicable and intended to be left unfilled, the signer should be asked to line through each space (using ink), or to write in "Not Applicable" or "N/A."

6. Scan the document.

Notaries are not required to read the documents they notarize. However, they should note certain important particulars about each document, such as its title, for recording in a journal. Notaries may also count and record the number of pages; this can show whether pages were later fraudulently added or removed.

7. Check the document's date.

For acknowledgments, the date of signing on the document must either precede or be the same as the date of the notarization but not follow it. For a jurat, the document signing date and the notarization date must be the same.

A document dated to follow the date on its notarial certificate risks rejection by a recorder who may question how the document could have been notarized before it was signed.

8. Keep a journal of notarial acts.

While not required by law, a journal record is a vital part of any notarial act. If a notarized document is lost or altered, or if the transaction is later challenged, the Notary's journal may be valuable evidence. It may protect the rights of parties to a transaction and help Notaries defend themselves against false accusations.

The *Governor's Reference Manual for Notaries* (published by the Florida Governor's office in 2001) recommends that Notaries record all of the pertinent details of a notarization in a journal: the date, time and type of notarization; the date and type of document; the signature, printed name and address of the signer; how this person was identified; and notarial fees charged, if any. Any other pertinent data, such as the representative capacity of the signer, may also be entered.

9. Complete the journal entry first.

The Notary should complete the journal entry *before* filling out the notarial certificate. This prevents a signer from leaving before the important public record of the notarization is made in the journal.

10. Make sure the document has notarial wording.

If a notarial certificate does not come with the document, the Notary must ask the document signer what type of notarization — acknowledgment, jurat or other — is required. The Notary may then type the appropriate notarial wording on the document or attach a preprinted "loose" certificate.

If the signer does not know what type of notarization is required, he or she should contact the document's issuing or receiving agency to determine this. This decision is never the Notary's to make unless the Notary is also an attorney.

11. Be attentive to details.

When filling out the certificate, the Notary needs to make sure that the venue correctly identifies the place of notarization; if the venue is preprinted and incorrect, the Notary should line through the incorrect state and/or county, write in the proper site of the notarization and initial and date the change.

Also, the Notary must pay attention to spaces on the notarial certificate that indicate the number and gender of the document signers, as well as how they were identified — for example, leave the plural "(s)" untouched or cross it out, as appropriate.

12. Affix your signature and seal properly.

Notaries should sign exactly the same name appearing on their commissioning papers. And they must never forget to affix their official seal — a common reason for rejection of a document by a recorder.

The seal should be placed as close to the Notary's signature as possible without overprinting it. To prevent illegibility, a notarial seal should not be affixed over wording, particularly over a signature.

13. Protect loose certificates.

If the Notary has to attach a notarial certificate, it must be securely stapled to the left margin of the document. Notaries can protect against the removal of such attachments by embossing them together with the documents and writing the particulars of the document to which the certificate is attached on the certificate. For example, the notation, "This certificate is attached to a 15-page partnership agreement between John Smith and Mary Doe, signed October 16, 2009," would deter fraudulent removal and reattachment of a loose certificate.

14. Don't give advice.

Every state prohibits nonattorneys from practicing law. Notaries should never prepare or complete documents for others or give advice on any matter relating to a document unless they are attorneys or professionals certified or licensed in a relevant area of expertise. The nonattorney Notary never chooses the type of certificate or notarization a document needs, since this decision can have important legal ramifications. The Notary could be held liable for any damages resulting from an incorrectly chosen certificate or notarization. ■

Notary Laws Explained

In layperson's language, this chapter discusses and clarifies key parts of the laws of Florida that regulate Notaries Public. These laws are reprinted in "Florida Laws Pertaining to Notaries Public" beginning on page 81.

Most provisions cited are from Chapter 117, "Notaries Public," of the Florida Statutes (FS). Other notarial rules are provided in the *Governor's Reference Manual for Notaries* (RMN), a guide for Notaries published by the Florida Governor's office.

THE NOTARY COMMISSION

Application for Commission

Qualifications. To become a Notary in Florida, the applicant must be a legal Florida resident at least 18 years old (FS 117.01[1]).

Mandatory Course. Within one year of applying, each first-time applicant must take and pass an interactive or classroom course on notarial duties of at least three hours from a private or public agency approved by the Governor's office. A certificate of course completion must be included with the application. Applicants renewing their commissions are not required to take another course (FS 668.50[11][b]).

Application. Each applicant must complete the official application provided by the Department of State. The application contains both the Notary's oath of office and the affidavit of good character (FS 117.01[2]).

Affidavit of Good Character. An affidavit attesting to the applicant's good character must be completed by someone unrelated to him or her who has known the applicant for at least one year. This affidavit is included on the Notary application form (FS 117.01[2]).

Application Fee. The total fee for a Notary commission applicant is $39 — $10 of which is the commission fee, $25 is the application fee and $4 a surcharge to be used by the Governor to educate and assist Notaries (FS 117.01[2]).

Permanent Residents. A permanent resident who applies for a Notary commission must also file with his or her application a recorded Declaration of Domicile (FS 117.01[1]).

Fictitious Names. An applicant may not submit a fictitious or assumed name except for a regularly used nickname on the application for commission (FS 117.01[2]).

Previous Convictions. If the Notary has indicated on the application that he or she has been convicted of a felony, a written statement describing the felony, along with a Certificate of Restoration of Civil Rights, must be submitted (FS 117.01[2]).

Application Misstatement. The Governor may suspend a Notary's commission for material false statements on the Notary Public application (FS 117.01[4]).

Notary Bond

Requirement. Every Florida Notary is required to obtain a bond of $7,500 payable to any person financially damaged as a result of the Notary's misconduct (FS 117.01[7][a]).

Filing the Bond. The bond must be filed with the Department of State with the commission application, the oath of office and affidavit of good character (FS 117.01[2]).

Surety. The surety for the Notary's bond must be a state-licensed bonding company. Notaries may not offer their own assets, or the assets of a friend, relative or employer, as a surety (FS 117.01[7][a]).

Claims. Whenever a claim is made against the Notary and any funds are paid out on his or her behalf, the bonding company must notify the Governor of the circumstances leading to the claim (FS 117.01[8]).

Protects Public. The Notary bond protects the public from a Notary's misconduct. The bond does not protect the Notary. The bond's surety is normally a bonding company that agrees to pay damages to anyone who suffers financially because of the Notary's improper acts, intentional or not, in the event that the Notary does not have the financial resources to pay these damages. The surety will seek compensation from the Notary for any damages it has to pay out on the Notary's behalf.

Liable for All Damages. A Notary and the surety company bonding the Notary may be sued by any person who has been damaged by the Notary's errors. The surety is liable only up to the amount of the bond ($7,500 in Florida), but a Notary may be found liable for any amount of money.

Oath of Office

Requirement. Every Florida Notary is required to take an official oath that he or she will honestly and faithfully carry out the duties of office. As part of the oath, the Notary must swear that he or she has read the laws regarding Notaries Public (FS 117.01–117.20) and knows the duties and responsibilities of being a Notary (FS 117.01[3] and [7][a]).

Filing the Oath. The oath is a written statement included on the application for commission. Since the statement is signed under penalties of perjury, signing the statement has the same effect as taking an oral oath (FS 117.01[2]).

Jurisdiction

Statewide. Notaries may perform official acts throughout the state of Florida but not beyond the state borders. A Notary may not witness a signing outside of Florida and then return to the state to perform the notarization. All parts of a notarial act must be performed at the same time and place within the state of Florida (FS 117.01[1]).

Term of Office

Four-Year Term. A Notary's term of office is four years, beginning with the date specified on the commission certificate and ending at midnight on the expiration date (FS 117.01[1]).

Reappointment

Procedure. No person will automatically be reappointed at the end of the four-year term. A Notary who wishes to renew his or her commission must complete the same application process as a new Notary (FS 117.01[6]).

Law Enforcement Officers

May Act as Notaries. Law enforcement and correctional officers, including probation officers, traffic accident investigators and traffic infraction enforcement officers, have the authority to act as Notaries Public whenever they are engaged in official duties. That is, they may take acknowledgments and administer oaths and affirmations; however, they may not perform marriages (FS 117.10).

Civil-Law Notaries

Qualifications. To qualify as a civil-law Notary, a person must be a member in good standing of the Florida Bar, have practiced law for at least five years and been appointed a civil-law Notary by the Department of State (FS 118.10).

For more information on becoming a civil-law Notary, contact the Department of State at (850) 245-6975 or the Florida Bar.

Authority. A civil-law Notary has all of the authority of a state-commissioned Notary Public but may also perform "authentic acts" which confirm the text of an instrument, the signatures of the transacting parties and the signature and seal of the civil-law Notary (FS 118.10).

The civil-law Notary may transact business and execute notarial acts for use in a jurisdiction outside of the United States unless the U.S. Department of State has determined that the particular jurisdiction does not have diplomatic relations with the United States or if trade with the specific jurisdiction is prohibited under the Trading with the Enemy Act of 1917 (50 U.S. Code, Sec. 1, et. seq.) (FS 118.10).

'Protocol' Required. Similar to the Notary's official journal of acts, a "protocol" is a register of all transactions performed by the civil-law Notary. A civil-law Notary's official acts are to be recorded in the protocol (FS 118.10).

Regulations. The Department of State may adopt regulations governing civil-law Notaries. However, the Department of State may not regulate, discipline or establish educational requirements for civil-law Notaries unless in agreement with the Florida Bar (FS 118.10).

Change of Address

Notification. Whenever a Notary changes the address or telephone number of his or her principal place of business or home, the Notary must inform the Department of State of the change. To act as a Florida Notary, the Notary must maintain state residency throughout the entire term of the appointment (FS 117.01[2]).

The Governor may suspend a Notary Public for failure to report a change of business or residence address or telephone number. The information must be submitted in writing within 60 days to the Department of State (FS 117.01[4][g]).

Moving Out of State. A Notary Public who moves out of state must resign the commission (FS 117.01[5][b]). (See "Resignation," below.)

Change of Name

Notification Required. A Notary who changes his or her name must file a name change form with the Secretary of State within 60 days of the change. The form shall include the new name and a specimen of the new signature. A rider to the Notary's bond, the old commission paper and a $25 fee must accompany the application. The Notary may continue to notarize in the old name until receipt of an amended commission — showing the new name — from the Department of State or the passage of 60 days, whichever comes first (FS 117.05[9]).

The Governor may suspend a Notary Public commission for failure to submit the required information to request an amended commission due to a name change (FS 117.01[4][g]).

Resignation

Required. Resignation is required when the Governor requires it, when a Notary fails to maintain residency in the state or when the Notary no longer wishes to act as a Notary (FS 117.01[5][b]).

Procedure. If a Notary Public wishes to resign the commission, he or she must send a signed letter of resignation to the Governor and include his or her original Notary commission certificate. Unless otherwise requested, the Notary Public must also destroy his or her seal and/or embosser (FS 117.01[5][b]).

Change of Criminal Record

Notification Required. Any conviction or other change in a Notary's criminal record must be reported to the Secretary of State within 60 days (FS 117.01[2]).

Lost or Misplaced Commission Certificate

A duplicate commission certificate of one that is lost or misplaced may be requested from the Department of State, Bureau of Notaries Public (RMN).

OFFICIAL NOTARIAL ACTS

Authorized Acts

Notaries may perform the following notarizations:

- Acknowledgments, certifying that a signer personally appeared before the Notary, was positively identified and acknowledged signing the document (FS 117.04). (See pages 23–28.)

- Certified Copies. A Notary may make or supervise the making of a photocopy of a document that is not a vital or public record and attest to the trueness of the copy (FS 117.05[12]). (See pages 28–30.)

- Inventorying a Safe-Deposit Box, certifying the contents of a safe-deposit box opened by a financial institution due to non-payment of rental fees (FS 655.94). (See pages 30–31.)

- Jurats, certifying that the signer personally appeared before the Notary, was positively identified, signed in the Notary's presence and took an oath or affirmation from the Notary (FS 117.05). (See pages 31–32.)

- Marriages. Florida Notaries are authorized to solemnize marriages as long as the couple presents a valid marriage certificate (FS 117.045). (See pages 32–34.)

- Oaths and Affirmations, which are solemn promises to a Supreme Being (oath) or solemn promises on one's own personal honor (affirmation) (FS 117.03). (See pages 34–36.)

- Verifying a Vehicle Identification Number, or VIN, by physical inspection (FS 319.23). (See pages 37–38.)

Unauthorized Acts

Proofs of Execution by Subscribing Witness. Although Florida statutes address the recording of documents proved by subscribing witness, the Florida Governor's office states that a proof of execution by subscribing witness is not a notarial act (FS 695.03 and 2001 RMN, p. 54). (See pages 36–37.)

Notary Named in Document. A Notary Public may not notarize a document in which the Notary's name appears as a party to the transaction (FS 117.107[12]).

Blank Certificates. A Notary may not sign and affix a seal to a blank notarial certificate and then deliver that certificate to another person for the purpose of notarization (FS 117.107[3]).

Certifying Copies of Vital or Public Records. A Notary is not authorized to certify a copy of a document that is a vital or public record (FS 117.05[12][a]).

Incomplete Documents. It is unlawful to notarize an incomplete document. This does not apply to a blank endorsement or assignment of a negotiable or nonnegotiable note, or of a document given as security for such a note (FS 117.107[10]).

Mentally Incapable of Understanding. A Notary may not notarize for a person who appears "mentally incapable of understanding" the document's effect (FS 117.107[5]), or for a person that the Notary knows has been ruled mentally incapacitated by a court (FS 117.107[4]).

Notary's Own Signature. A Notary is not permitted to notarize his or her own signature (FS 117.107[12]).

Notarization Without Appearance. A Notary may not notarize the signature of a person who does not personally appear before the Notary at the time of notarization. A Notary who violates this law is guilty of a civil infraction and can be fined up to $5,000 regardless of whether the Notary had fraudulent intentions (FS 117.107[9]).

Notarizing for Relatives. A Notary may not notarize for a spouse, son, daughter, mother or father (FS 117.107[11]).

Signing False Names. A Notary may not sign a notarial certificate using any name other than the one under which he or she was commissioned (FS 117.107[1]).

Acknowledgments

A Common Notarial Act. Acknowledgments are one of the most common forms of notarization. Typically, they are executed on documents such as deeds and liens affecting the title to real property that will be publicly recorded by a county recorder.

Purpose. In executing an acknowledgment, the Notary certifies three things (FS 117.05[4]–[5]):

1) The signer *personally appeared* before the Notary on the date and in the county indicated on the notarial certificate (notarization cannot be based upon a telephone call or a Notary's familiarity with a signature).

2) The signer was *positively identified* by the Notary through either personal knowledge or satisfactory evidence (see "Identifying Document Signers," page 38).

3) The signer *acknowledged* to the Notary that the signature was freely made for the purposes stated in the document. (If a document is willingly signed in the presence of the Notary, this can serve just as well as an oral statement of acknowledgment.)

Certificate for Acknowledgment. For every acknowledgment, the Notary must complete a notarial certificate that includes a statement as to how the signer was identified and that the signer personally appeared before the Notary (FS 117.05[4]). (See "Notary Certificate," pages 45–47.)

Florida law provides certificate wording for acknowledgments by persons signing in individual and representative capacities. The authorization of these forms does not prohibit the use of other appropriate wordings (FS 117.05[13][b][c]).

- Individual Acknowledgment — for an individual signing on his or her own behalf:

State of Florida

County of _____

The foregoing instrument was acknowledged before me this _____ day of _____ (month), _____ (year), by _____ (name of person acknowledging).

_____ (Signature of Notary)   (Seal of Notary)

_____ (Name of Notary, printed, typed or stamped)

Personally known _____ OR produced identification _____

Type of identification produced _____

- Representative Acknowledgment Certificate — for a corporate officer, trustee, executor, attorney in fact, guardian or other representative acting on behalf of an entity or person:

State of Florida

County of _____

The foregoing instrument was acknowledged before me this _____ day of _____ (month), _____ (year), by _____ (name of person) as _____ (type of authority, e.g. officer, trustee, attorney in fact) for _____ (name of party on behalf of whom instrument was executed).

_____ (Signature of Notary)   (Seal of Notary)

_____ (Name of Notary, printed, typed or stamped)

Personally known _____ OR produced identification _____

Type of identification produced _____

Short-Form Acknowledgment Certificates.* In addition to the preceding certificates, Florida law authorizes the use of several short-form certificates that accommodate signers in various representative capacities. The authorization of these short forms does not prohibit the use of other suitable forms (FS 695.25).

---

* For short-form acknowledgment certificates, Florida law specifies that the title or rank and the serial number of the officer be included. This requirement appears to be directed at non-Notary officers, since the Notary's seal contains this information.

- Individual Acknowledgment Short-Form Certificate — for an individual or individuals signing on his or her behalf:

State of Florida
County of _____

The foregoing instrument was acknowledged before me this _____ (date) by _____ (name of person acknowledging), who is personally known to me or who has produced _____ (type of identification) as identification.

_____ (Signature of Notary)   (Seal of Notary)
_____ (Name of Notary, printed, typed or stamped)

- Corporate Acknowledgment Short-Form Certificate — for a corporate officer acting on behalf of a corporation:

State of Florida
County of _____

The foregoing instrument was acknowledged before me this _____ (date) by _____ (name of officer or agent, title of officer or agent) of _____ (name of corporation acknowledging), a _____ (state or place of incorporation) corporation, on behalf of the corporation. He/she is personally known to me or has produced _____ (type of identification) as identification.

_____ (Signature of Notary)   (Seal of Notary)
_____ (Name of Notary, printed, typed or stamped)

- Partnership Acknowledgment Short-Form Certificate — for a partner or partners acting on behalf of a partnership:

State of Florida
County of _____

The foregoing instrument was acknowledged before me this _____ (date) by _____ (name of acknowledging partner or agent), partner (or agent) on behalf of _____ (name of partnership), a partnership. He/she is personally known to me or has produced _____(type of identification) as identification.

_____ (Signature of Notary)   (Seal of Notary)
_____ (Name of Notary, printed, typed or stamped)

- Attorney in Fact Acknowledgment Short-Form Certificate —
for an attorney in fact acting on behalf of a principal:

State of Florida

County of _____

The foregoing instrument was acknowledged before me this _____
(date) by _____ (name of attorney in fact) as attorney in fact, who
is personally known to me or who has produced _____ (type of
identification) as identification on behalf of _____ (Name of principal).

_____ (Signature of Notary)   (Seal of Notary)

_____ (Name of Notary, printed, typed or stamped)

- Representative Acknowledgment Short-Form Certificate — for
a public officer, trustee, executor, administrator, guardian or
other representative acting on behalf of an entity or person:

State of Florida

County of _____

The foregoing instrument was acknowledged before me this _____ (date)
by _____ (name and title of position), who is personally known to
me or who has produced _____ (type of identification) as identification.

_____ (Signature of Notary)   (Seal of Notary)

_____ (Name of Notary, printed, typed or stamped)

Identification of Acknowledger. In an acknowledgment, the
Notary must identify the signer either through personal knowledge,
credible identifying witness(es) or identification documents (FS
117.05[5]). (See "Identifying Document Signers," page 38.)

Witnessing Signature Not Required. For an acknowledgment,
the document does not have to be signed in the Notary's
presence. Rather, the document signer need only acknowledge
having made the signature. The document could have been
signed an hour before, a week before, a year before, etc. As long
as the signer appears before the Notary at the time of notarization
to *acknowledge having signed*, the Notary may execute the
acknowledgment. (However, for a jurat notarization requiring an
oath or affirmation, the document must be signed in the presence
of the Notary. See "Jurats," pages 31–32.)

Out-of-State Acknowledgments. Acknowledgment certificates completed outside of Florida by Notaries of another state in accordance with the laws of that state may be recorded in Florida. However, acknowledgments completed in Florida for use out of the state must substantially comply with the wording prescribed in the Florida Statutes, Sections 117.05[13] or 695.25.

Terminology. In discussing the notarial act of acknowledgment, it is important to use the proper terminology. A Notary takes or executes an acknowledgment, while a document signer makes or gives an acknowledgment.

Who May Take. In addition to Notaries, the following officials may take acknowledgments within the state of Florida (FS 695.03):

1) A civil-law Notary of Florida.

2) A judge, clerk or deputy clerk of any court.

3) A United States commissioner or magistrate.

Outside of Florida, but within the United States and its jurisdictions, acknowledgments may be executed by (FS 695.03):

1) A Notary Public of the state or jurisdiction.

2) A Florida civil-law Notary or a commissioner of deeds appointed by the Florida governor.

3) A judge or clerk of any court of the United States, or of any state, territory or district.

4) A U.S. commissioner or magistrate.

5) A justice of the peace, master in chancery or registrar or recorder of deeds in any state, territory or district having a seal.

Outside of United States jurisdictions, acknowledgments may be executed by (FS 695.03):

1) A Notary Public of the foreign jurisdiction.

2) A Florida civil-law Notary or a commissioner of deeds appointed by the Florida Governor.

3) An ambassador, envoy, minister, commissioner, charge d'affaires, consul general, consul, vice consul, consular agent or other U.S. consular officer in the foreign jurisdiction.

4) A U.S. military or naval officer authorized to perform the duties of a Notary Public.

Certified Copies

Purpose. Florida Notaries have the authority to certify — or "attest" — that a copy of an original document is a complete and true reproduction of the document that was copied. The Notary's authority to certify copies is limited to documents that are not vital records or public records, if a copy can be made by the custodian of the public record (FS 117.05[12][a]).

Procedure. The permanent custodian of the original document must present it to the Notary and request a certified copy. The Notary must make or closely supervise the making of the photocopy to ensure that it is true, exact and unaltered (FS 117.05[12][a]).

A common request is to certify a copy of a college diploma, since only one such document exists and most people do not want to part with the original when proof of their graduate status is requested by a prospective employer or school.

Examples of the documents that may be lawfully photocopied and certified by a Florida Notary are: a Florida driver's license, a vehicle title, a Social Security card, a medical record, a passport, a bill of sale, a contract or a lease.

Precautions. Florida law permits Notaries to certify only photocopies of original documents, never hand-rendered reproductions. To minimize the opportunity for fraud, the making of the photocopy should be done by the Notary. Otherwise, the Notary should carefully compare the copy to the original, word for word, to ensure that it is complete and identical.

Copy Certification of Recordable Documents Prohibited. Florida Notaries are prohibited from certifying copies of recordable documents. An individual who needs a certified copy of a recordable document such as a deed should first record the document and then have the recording agency provide a certified copy (FS 117.05[12][a]).

Copy Certification of Vital Records Prohibited. Florida Notaries are expressly prohibited from certifying copies of birth or death certificates, because these are vital records. Only officials in a bureau of vital statistics or other public record office may certify originals or copies of such certificates. (See "Bureaus of Vital Statistics," pages 108–111.) A Notary's "certification" of such a copy may lend credibility to what is actually a counterfeit or altered document (FS 117.05[12][a]).

Certified Copy Certificate. Attesting to the trueness of a copy should substantially comply with the following (FS 117.05[12][b]):

State of Florida

County of _____

On this the _____ day of _____ (month), _____ (year), I attest that the preceding or attached document is a true, exact, complete and unaltered photocopy made by me of _____ (description of document), presented to me by the document's custodian, _____, and, to the best of my knowledge, that the photocopied document is neither a vital record nor a public record, certified copies of which are available from an official source other than a Notary Public.

_____ (Signature of Notary)   (Seal of Notary)
_____ (Name of Notary, printed, typed or stamped)

Copies of Notarial Records

Written Request. If an individual desires a copy of a journal entry or other notarial record, it is recommended that the Notary require a written and signed request that specifies the name(s) of the party(ies) whose signature(s) was/were notarized, the type of document and the month and year of the notarization.

Certificate for Certified Copy of Notarial Record. The National Notary Association recommends the following certificate wording for certifying a copy of an entry or page from the Notary's journal or other notarial record:

State of Florida

County of _____

On this _____ day of _____ (month), _____ (year), I, _____
(name of Notary Public), the undersigned Notary Public, hereby declare that
the attached reproduction of a Notary journal entry involving _____
(describe document, noting date and signers) is a true and correct photocopy
made from a page in my Notary journal.

_____ (Signature of Notary)   (Seal of Notary)

_____ (Name of Notary, printed, typed or stamped)

Inventorying a Safe-Deposit Box

Purpose. Florida law allows financial institutions, such as
banks, to open a safe-deposit box if the rental fees are overdue,
attempts have been made to notify the renter and no response
has been received. A Notary Public is required to be present for
the opening, to inventory the contents of the box and to complete
a certificate as evidence (FS 655.94[1]).

Procedure. Both a Notary and an officer of the institution must
be present at the time the safe-deposit box is opened. When the
box is opened, the Notary must inventory the contents of the
box and complete a certificate detailing the items discovered (FS
655.94[1]).

Journal Signature. If the Notary keeps a journal of notarial acts,
it is recommended that the Notary obtain the signature of the
officer and any witnesses as well.

Certificate for Inventorying a Safe-Deposit Box. The Notary's
certificate should include the name of the lessee, the date of
opening and a list of the contents. A copy of the certificate should
be given to the institution, and the original should be placed in
the package containing the contents (FS 655.94[1]).

Florida law does not provide specific wording for the
certificate. The *Governor's Reference Manual for Notaries* suggests
the following form:

State of Florida

County of _____

On the _____ day of _____ (month), _____ (year), safe-deposit box number _____, rented in the name of _____, was opened by _____ (name of financial institution) in my presence and in the presence of _____ (name of officer). The contents of the box consisted of the following:

(list of contents)

_____ (Signature of bank officer)

_____ (Print or type name)

_____ (Signature of person opening box)

_____ (Print or type name)

_____ (Signature of Notary)   (Seal of Notary)

_____ (Name of Notary, printed, typed or stamped)

Jurats

Part of Verification. In notarizing affidavits, depositions and other forms of written verification requiring an oath by the signer, the Notary normally executes a jurat.

Purpose. While the purpose of an acknowledgment is to positively identify a document signer, the purpose of a verification with jurat is to compel truthfulness by appealing to the signer's conscience and fear of criminal penalties for perjury.

In executing a jurat, a Notary certifies that (FS 117.05):

1) The signer *personally appeared* before the Notary at the time of notarization on the date and in the county indicated (notarization based upon a telephone call or on familiarity with a signature is not acceptable).

2) The signer was *positively identified* by the Notary through either personal knowledge or satisfactory evidence. (See "Identifying Document Signers," page 38.)

3) The Notary *witnessed the signature* being made at the time of notarization.

4) The Notary *administered an oath (or affirmation)* to the signer.

Certificate for a Jurat. A jurat is the wording, "Subscribed and sworn to (or affirmed) before me on this _____ (date) by _____ (name of signer) ..." or similar language. The following wording is prescribed by Florida law (FS 117.05[13][a]):

State of Florida

County of _____

Sworn to (or affirmed) and subscribed before me this _____ day of
_____ (month), _____ (year), by _____ (name of signer).

_____ (Signature of Notary)   (Seal of Notary)

_____ (Name of Notary, printed, typed or stamped)

Personally known _____ OR produced identification _____

Type of identification produced _____

Wording for Jurat Oath (Affirmation). If not otherwise
prescribed, a Florida Notary may use the following or similar
wording to administer an oath (or affirmation) with a jurat:

> Do you solemnly swear that the statements in this document are true to the
> best of your knowledge and belief, so help you God?

> (Do you solemnly affirm that the statements in this document are true to the
> best of your knowledge and belief?)

Marriages

Authority. Florida is one of only a few U.S. states that allow
Notaries to perform marriages. Maine, South Carolina and one
parish in Louisiana are the others. Unless the Notary is also a
clergy member, the Notary-performed marriage is a civil ceremony
(FS 117.045 and 741.07[1]).

Procedure. The Notary must ensure that the couple present a
valid marriage license from a county court judge or clerk of the
circuit court. The Notary may then perform the ceremony within
the boundaries of the state (2001 RMN, p. 16).

Ceremony.* The Secretary of State does not recommend
wording for the ceremony. The Notary may personalize it, or the
bride and groom may exchange their own vows. The couple's
vows must reflect their binding commitment to one another.

In a typical ceremony, the man stands on the woman's right,
and the Notary speaks the following words (2001 RMN, p. 16):

---

* Page 116 includes a sample marriage ceremony in Spanish.

Dearly beloved, we are gathered here today (tonight) to join this man and this woman in (holy) matrimony.

The Notary asks the man:

_____ (man's name), do you take this woman to be your lawful wedded wife, to live together in (holy) matrimony, to love, honor, comfort her and keep her in sickness and in health, and forsaking all others, for as long as you both shall live?

The man answers, "I do," and the Notary asks the woman:

_____ (woman's name), do you take this man to be your lawful wedded husband, to live together in (holy) matrimony, to love, honor, comfort him and keep him in sickness and in health, and forsaking all others, for as long as you both shall live?

The woman answers, "I do." The Notary then asks the man to repeat the following:

I, _____ (man's name), take you, _____ (woman's name) to be my wife, to have and to hold from this day forward, for better, for worse, for richer, for poorer, in sickness and in health, to love and to cherish, till death do us part.

The woman also repeats:

I, _____ (woman's name), take you, _____ (man's name) to be my husband, to have and to hold from this day forward, for better, for worse, for richer, for poorer, in sickness and in health, to love and to cherish, till death do us part.

If the couple has a ring, the Notary asks the man to place it on the woman's finger and they both repeat the following:

I give you this ring as a token and pledge of our constant faith and abiding love.

After the ring has been given, the Notary asks the couple to join hands and declares:

Inasmuch as _____ (man) and _____ (woman) have this day consented to be joined in (holy) wedlock and have given and pledged their troth each to the other in the presence of this company, by virtue of the authority vested me under the laws of the State of Florida, I now pronounce you husband and wife. The bride and groom may now kiss.

Certificate for Marriage. Finally, the Notary is responsible for completing the certificate on the appropriate portion of the marriage license. The Notary must then return the license to the office of the county court judge or clerk of the circuit court that issued the license within 10 days after the marriage is performed (FS 741.08).

Relatives. Notaries may perform marriage ceremonies for relatives. The statute prohibiting notarizing for a son, daughter, mother or father does not apply to this situation because the Notary is not notarizing the signature of the bride and groom. He or she is merely certifying that the couple has been joined in matrimony according to Florida law (1991 Florida Attorney General's Opinion 91-70).

Fees. For solemnizing the rites of matrimony, a Notary Public may charge the same fee that clerks of the circuit court can charge for like services: $30 (FS 117.045 and 28.24[29]).

Oaths and Affirmations

Purpose. An oath is a solemn, spoken pledge to a Supreme Being. An affirmation is a solemn, spoken pledge on one's own personal honor, with no reference to a Supreme Being. Both are usually promises of truthfulness and have the same legal effect.

In taking an oath or affirmation in an official proceeding, a person may be subject to criminal penalties for perjury should he or she fail to be truthful.

An oath or affirmation can be a full-fledged notarial act in its own right, as when giving an oath of office to a public official (when "swearing in" a public official), or it can be part of the process of notarizing a document (e.g., executing a jurat or swearing in a subscribing witness).

A person who objects to taking an oath may instead be given an affirmation.

Power to Administer. Florida Notaries and certain other officers are authorized to administer and complete certificates for oaths and affirmations (FS 117.03).

An acknowledgment is not an acceptable substitution for an oath. A Notary may not take an acknowledgment in lieu of an oath if an oath is required (FS 117.03).

<u>Wording for Oath (Affirmation)</u>. If law does not dictate otherwise, a Florida Notary may use the following or similar words in administering an oath (or affirmation):

- Oath (Affirmation) for affiant signing an affidavit:

Do you solemnly swear that the statements in this document are true to the best of your knowledge and belief, so help you God?

(Do you solemnly affirm that the statements in this document are true to the best of your knowledge and belief?)

- Oath (Affirmation) for witness testifying in a court case:

Do you solemnly swear that the evidence you shall give in this issue (or matter), pending between (first party) and (second party), shall be the truth, the whole truth and nothing but the truth, so help you God?

(Do you solemnly affirm that the evidence you shall give in this issue [or matter], pending between [first party] and [second party], shall be the truth, the whole truth and nothing but the truth?)

- Oath (Affirmation) for credible identifying witness:

Do you solemnly swear that (person making the acknowledgment) is the person named in the document; that (person making the acknowledgment) is personally known to you; that it is your reasonable belief that the circumstances of (person making the acknowledgment) are such that it would be very difficult or impossible for him/her to obtain another form of identification; that (person making the acknowledgment) does not possess any of the acceptable identification documents; and that you do not have a financial interest nor are you named in the document being acknowledged, so help you God?

(Do you solemnly affirm that [person making the acknowledgment] is the person named in the document; that [person making the acknowledgment] is personally known to you; that it is your reasonable belief that the circumstances of [person making the acknowledgment] are such that it would be very difficult or impossible for him/her to obtain another form of identification; that [person making the acknowledgment] does not possess any of the acceptable identification documents; and that you do not have a financial interest nor are you named in the document being acknowledged?)

In addition to administering the oath or affirmation to a credible identifying witness, the Notary must obtain a sworn, written statement from that witness. (See pages 40–41.)

<u>Response Required</u>. The oath or affirmation wording must be spoken aloud, and the person taking the oath or affirmation must answer affirmatively with, "I do," "Yes" or the like. A nod or grunt is not a clear and sufficient response. If a person is unable to speak, the Notary may rely upon written notes to communicate.

<u>Ceremony and Gestures</u>. To impress upon the oath-taker or affirmant the importance of truthfulness, the Notary is encouraged to lend a sense of ceremony and formality to the oath or affirmation. During the administration of an oath or affirmation, the Notary and document signer traditionally raise their right hands, though this is not a legal requirement. Notaries generally have discretion to use words and gestures they feel will most compellingly appeal to the conscience of the oath-taker or affirmant.

Proof of Execution by Subscribing Witness

<u>In Lieu of Acknowledgment</u>. In many states, but not in Florida, a proof of execution by subscribing witness is regarded as an acceptable substitute for an acknowledgment on a recordable real estate document.

<u>Subscribing Witness</u>. A subscribing witness is a person who watches a principal sign a document and then subscribes (signs) his or her own name on the document at the principal's request. This witness brings that document to an authorized officer on the principal's behalf and takes an oath or affirmation from the officer to the effect that the principal did willingly sign the document and request the witness to also sign the document.

The ideal subscribing witness personally knows the principal signer and has no personal beneficial or financial interest in the document or transaction. It would be foolish of the officer taking the proof, for example, to rely upon the word of a subscribing witness presenting for notarization a power of attorney that names this very witness as attorney in fact.

Because of the high potential for fraud with this type of notarization, the subscribing witness should be personally known to the officer taking the proof. Also allowed, but less preferred, is identification of the subscribing witness through either a credible identifying witness (or witnesses) or approved identification documents.

Florida Prohibits Non-Appearance Notarizations. Though FS 695.03 does recognize proofs, according to the *Governor's Reference Manual for Notaries*, a proof of execution by a subscribing witness is not allowed in Florida because the principal signer must always appear before the Notary. "Remember, then, if a co-worker, family member or anyone else asks you to notarize another person's signature based upon a sworn statement that he or she saw the person sign the document, JUST SAY NO!!" (2001 RMN, p. 54).

However, a procedure is prescribed by FS 695.03(1) whereby a signed real estate document lacking notarization whose signer is not locatable or deceased may be prepared for recordation by the "proof" of one of the subscribing witnesses. In such a rare circumstance, the Notary would notarize a "certificate of proof" or an affidavit of proof signed by the witness using a standard jurat (2001 RMN, p. 54).

Verifying a Vehicle Identification Number

Purpose. When a person applies for a Florida title on a used motor vehicle, a physical inspection must be done by an individual authorized to certify a vehicle identification number (VIN). Florida law authorizes a Notary to make such a certification. The owner of the vehicle must swear before a Notary that the VIN and odometer reading are correct (FS 319.23[3][a][2]).

State officials explain that the Florida Department of Highway Safety and Motor Vehicles has issued new title forms to be used for new vehicles. These new forms do not require notarization, and the Department has omitted the notarial wording from the form. However, older title forms which do require notarization are still in circulation on older and used vehicles. Therefore, the Notary should be aware of the differences and understand how to notarize the older forms if presented by a signer.

Verification Form. Both the owner's declaration and the Notary's verification are included on a form provided by the Department of Highway Safety and Motor Vehicles.

Part A of the form is used for the owner's sworn statement pertaining to the VIN and odometer reading. In this section, the Notary simply executes a jurat, meaning that the owner must take an oath and sign in the Notary's presence. Part B of the form requires the Notary to perform a physical inspection of the vehicle for the purpose of verifying that the vehicle's identification number is the same as the number on the form. This part of the form must also be signed, sealed and dated by the Notary (2001 RMN, p. 17).

PRACTICES AND PROCEDURES

Identifying Document Signers

Procedure. In notarizing any signature, whether by acknowledgment or jurat, Florida law requires the Notary to positively identify the document signer. The following three methods of identification are acceptable (FS 117.05[5]):

1) The Notary's *personal knowledge* of the signer's identity (see "Personal Knowledge of Identity," pages 38-39);

2) Reliable *identification documents* or ID cards (see "Identification Documents [ID Cards]," pages 39–40); or

3) The oath or affirmation of one personally known *credible identifying witness* or two *credible identifying witnesses* identified by identification documents (see "Credible Identifying Witness[es]," pages 40–43).

Indicate on Notarial Certificate. The Notary must indicate on the certificate of acknowledgment or jurat the method of identification of the signer — that is, whether the Notary relied upon personal knowledge or satisfactory evidence and the type of evidence produced (FS 117.05[5]).

Personal Knowledge of Identity

Definition. The safest and most reliable method of identifying a document signer is for the Notary to depend upon his or her own personal knowledge of the signer's identity. Personal knowledge means familiarity with an individual resulting from interactions with that person over a period of time sufficient to eliminate every reasonable doubt that the person has the identity claimed. The familiarity should come from association with the individual in relation to other people and should be based upon a chain of circumstances surrounding the individual (FS 117.05[5][a]).

Florida law does not specify how long a Notary must be acquainted with an individual before personal knowledge of identity may be claimed. The Notary's common sense must prevail. In general, the longer the Notary is acquainted with a person, and the more interactions that the Notary has had with that person, the more likely the individual is personally known.

For instance, the Notary might safely regard a friend since childhood as personally known, but would be foolish to consider a person met for the first time the previous day as such. Whenever the Notary has a reasonable doubt about a signer's identity, that individual should not be considered personally known and the identification should be made through either a credible identifying witness or reliable identification documents.

Identification Documents (ID Cards)

Acceptable Identification Documents. A Notary may identify a document signer through any one of the identification documents listed below. The document must 1) be current or if expired, issued within the past five years, and 2) bear a serial or other identifying number (FS 117.05[5][b][2]):

- Florida driver's license or identification card issued by the Department of Highway Safety and Motor Vehicles.

- U.S. passport issued by the U.S. Department of State.

- Foreign passport if stamped by the U.S. Citizenship and Immigration Services (USCIS).

- Driver's license or non-driver's ID issued by another U.S. state or territory.

- Driver's license officially issued in Mexico or Canada.

- U.S. military ID.

- Inmate ID issued on or after January 1, 1991, by the Florida Department of Corrections or Federal Bureau of Prisons (but only to identify prisoners in custody).

- A sworn, written statement from a sworn law enforcement officer explaining that an inmate's IDs were confiscated upon incarceration, and that the person named in the document is the person whose signature is to be notarized.

- An identification card issued by U.S. Citizenship and Immigration Services (USCIS). The most common is the Permanent Resident ID, or "green card."

Unacceptable Identification Documents. Unacceptable ID cards for identifying acknowledgers include, but are not limited to: birth certificates, Social Security cards, credit cards and driver's licenses without photographs.

Multiple Identification. While one good identification document or card may be sufficient to identify a signer, the Notary may ask for more.

Credible Identifying Witness(es)

Purpose. When a document signer is not personally known to the Notary and is not able to present reliable identification documents, that signer may be identified through the oath (or affirmation) of one or two credible identifying witnesses (FS 117.05[5][b]).

Qualifications and Identification. Every credible identifying witness must personally know the document signer. If there is only one credible identifying witness to identify the signer, that witness must also be personally known by the Notary. This establishes a chain of personal knowledge from the signer to the credible identifying witness to the Notary.

If there are two credible identifying witnesses available to identify the signer, these witnesses need not be personally known to the Notary but must be identified through an acceptable identification document listed under "Identification Documents (ID Cards)," pages 39–40 (FS 117.05[5][b]).

Oath (Affirmation) for Credible Identifying Witness. To ensure truthfulness, the Notary must obtain a sworn, written statement from each credible identifying witness that the person signing the document is the person named in the document and that the signer is personally known to the witness (FS 117.05[5][b][1]).

If two credible identifying witnesses are used, the witnesses must swear (or affirm) in their statements that the following are true (FS 117.05[5][b][1]):

1) The person whose signature is to be notarized is the person named in the document.

2) The person whose signature is to be notarized is personally known to the witness.

3) That it is the reasonable belief of the witness that it would be very difficult or impossible for the person whose signature is to be notarized to obtain another form of identification.

4) The person whose signature is to be notarized does not possess any of the acceptable identification documents.

5) The witness does not have a financial interest in the document and is not named in the document.

<u>Written Statement</u>. If there is space on the document, the credible identifying witness's statement may be typed on the notarized document itself. If the statement is on a separate sheet of paper, the Notary should keep it for his or her records.

The Governor's Reference Manual for Notaries suggests the following wording for one credible identifying witness:

Under penalty of perjury, I declare that the person appearing before
_____ (name of Notary) is personally known to me as _____
(name of person whose signature is to be notarized) and is the person named
in the document requiring notarization.

_____ (Date)

_____ (Signature of witness)

State of Florida

County of _____

Sworn to and subscribed before me this _____ day of _____ (month),
_____ (year), by _____ (name of witness) who is personally known to me.

_____ (Signature of Notary)   (Seal of Notary)

_____ (Name of Notary, printed, typed or stamped)

Wording for two credible identifying witnesses should be substantially as follows (2001 RMN, p. 33):

Under the penalties of perjury, I declare that the person appearing before
_____ (name of Notary) is personally known to me as _____
(name of person whose signature is to be notarized) and is the person named
in the document requiring notarization; that I believe that this person does
not possess the required identification; that I believe it would be difficult or

impossible for this person to obtain such identification; and that I do not have a financial interest in and am not a party to the underlying transaction.

_____ (Date)
_____ (Signature of first witness)

_____ (Date)
_____ (Signature of second witness)

State of Florida

County of _____

Sworn to and subscribed before me this _____ day of _____ (month), _____ (year), by _____ (name of witness) who has produced _____ (type of identification) as identification, and by _____ (name of witness) who produced _____ (type of identification) as identification

_____ (Signature of Notary)   (Seal of Notary)
_____ (Name of Notary, printed, typed or stamped)

Signature in Notary's Journal. The prudent Notary will record the name, address and signature of each credible identifying witness in a journal. The Notary should also indicate how the witness was identified, either by the Notary's personal knowledge (required for one credible identifying witness) or through acceptable identification documents (required for two credible identifying witnesses).

Indicate on Certificate. The Notary must indicate in the certificate the method used to identify the signer. To indicate reliance upon a credible identifying witness or witnesses, the Notary should select the phrase "Produced Identification," and after "Type of Identification Produced" write in "credible identifying witness(es)" (FS 117.05[5]).

Not a Subscribing Witness. Do not confuse *credible identifying witnesses* with *subscribing witnesses.* A credible identifying witness vouches for the identity of a signer who appears before the Notary. A subscribing witness vouches for the genuineness of the signature of a person who does not appear before the Notary. (See "Proof of Execution by Subscribing Witness," pages 36–37.)

Journal of Notarial Acts

Recommendation. Both the National Notary Association and the Notary Section of the Governor's office recommend that every Notary keep a detailed, accurate and sequential journal of notarial acts even though it is not required by law (2001 RMN, pp. 42–43).

A journal record of a transaction demonstrates that the Notary used reasonable care in identifying a document signer. Failure to keep a journal, while not unlawful, can cause problems for a Notary if a transaction is challenged for any reason. A permanently bound recordbook (not loose-leaf) with numbered pages and entry spaces is best for preserving the sequence of notarial acts and for protecting against unauthorized removal of pages or tampering.

Journal Entries. For each notarization, the following vital information should be recorded (2001 RMN, p. 42):

1) The date, time of day, and type of notarization (e.g., jurat, acknowledgment, etc.).

2) The date and type of document notarized (e.g., deed of trust, affidavit of support, etc.).

3) The printed name, address and the signature of each person whose signature is notarized; the signature of any credible witness; and the signature of any witnesses to a signature by mark.

4) A statement as to how the signer's identity was confirmed. If by personal knowledge, the journal entry should read "Personal Knowledge." If by satisfactory evidence, the journal entry should contain either: a description of the ID card accepted, including the type of ID, the government agency issuing the ID, the serial or identifying number and the date of issuance or expiration; or the signature of each credible identifying witness and how the credible identifying witness was identified. (See "Credible Identifying Witness[es]," pages 40–42.)

5) The fee charged for the notarial service.

Additional Entries. Notaries may include additional information in the journal that is pertinent to a given notarization. Many

Notaries, for example, enter the telephone number of all signers and witnesses, as well as the address where the notarization was performed, if not at the Notary's office. A description of the document signer's demeanor (e.g., "The signer appeared very nervous") or notations about the identity of other persons who were present for the notarization may also be included.

One important entry to include is the signer's representative capacity — whether the signer is acting as attorney in fact, trustee, guardian, corporate officer or in another capacity — if not signing on his or her own behalf.

Increasingly, Notaries are asking document signers to leave a thumbprint in the journal as a deterrent to fraud, since no forger wants to leave a print behind as evidence of an attempted crime.

Since a journal record of a notarial act is not required by law, refusal to leave any of the above information is not sufficient grounds for the Notary to refuse to honor an otherwise lawful and reasonable request for a notarization.

Journal-Entry Copies. A Notary's official journal is a public record. Accordingly, if any person submits a written request specifying the month and year of a particular notarization, as well as the type of document and the names of the signers, the Notary may provide that person with a photocopy of the particular entry in the journal — but of no other entries! Adjacent entries should be covered by a sheet of blank paper before the photocopy is made. (See "Copies of Notarial Records," page 29-30.)

The National Notary Association discourages "fishing expeditions" through the Notary journal by persons who are not able to be specific about the entry sought.

Never Surrender Journal. Notaries should never surrender control of their journals to anyone, unless subpoenaed by a court order. Even when an employer has paid for the Notary's journal and seal, they go with the Notary upon termination of employment; no person but the Notary can lawfully possess and use these official adjuncts of office (FS 117.05[3][e]).

Notary Certificate

Requirement. In notarizing any document, a Notary must complete a notarial certificate. The certificate is wording that indicates exactly what the Notary has certified. The Notary certificate may either be on the document itself or on an attachment to it (a "loose" certificate). The certificate should contain (FS 117.05[4]):

1) A *venue* indicating where the notarization is being performed. "State of Florida, County of _____," is the typical venue wording, with the county name inserted in the blank. The letters "SS." or "SCT." sometimes appear after the venue; they abbreviate the traditional Latin word scilicet, meaning "in particular" or "namely."

2) A *statement of particulars* which indicates what the notarization has attested to. An acknowledgment certificate would include such wording as: "On _____ (date) before me, _____ (name of Notary), personally appeared, _____ (name of signer), personally known to me (or proved to me on the basis of satisfactory evidence) to be the person(s) ... etc." A jurat certificate would include such wording as: "Subscribed and sworn to (or affirmed) before me this _____ (date) by _____ (name of signer)."

3) A *testimonium* clause, which may be optional if the date is included in the statement of particulars: "Witness my hand and official seal, this the _____ day of _____ (month), ____ (year)." In this short sentence, the Notary formally attests to the truthfulness of the preceding facts in the certificate. "Hand" means signature.

4) The *official signature of the Notary,* exactly as the name appears on the commissioning paper. A facsimile signature stamp may not be used unless the Notary has a physical disability that prevents or limits signing and the Department of State is notified in writing and given a sample facsimile (FS 117.107[2]).

5) The *official seal of the Notary.* On many certificates the letters "L.S." appear, indicating where the seal is to be located. These letters abbreviate the Latin term locus sigilli, meaning "place of the seal." The inking seal should be placed near but not over the letters, so that wording imprinted by the seal will not be obscured. An embossing seal, used in conjunction with an inking seal, may be placed directly over the letters — slightly displacing portions of the

characters and leaving a clue that document examiners can use to distinguish an original from a forged photocopy.

In addition to the basic elements described above, a notarial certificate must also indicate the following (FS 117.05[4]):

• That the signer personally appeared before the Notary at the time of notarization.

• The exact date of the notarial act.

• The name of the person whose signature is being notarized.

• The manner in which the signer was identified.

Loose Certificates. When certificate wording is not preprinted on the document for the Notary to fill out, a loose certificate may be attached, provided that the signer indicates the type of notarial wording needed. Under no circumstances should a nonattorney Notary decide what type of certificate to attach, because this could be considered the unauthorized practice of law. That decision must be made by the document signer, the document's issuing agency or its receiving agency.

Normally, the loose certificate is stapled to the document's left margin on the last page of the document. Only one side of the certificate should be stapled, so it can be lifted to view the document beneath it.

To prevent a loose certificate from being removed and fraudulently placed on another document, there are precautions a Notary can take. The Notary can emboss the certificate and document together, writing, "Attached document bears embossment," on the certificate. The Notary can also write a brief description of the document on the certificate: e.g., "This certificate is attached to a _____ (title or type of document), dated _____, of _____ (number) pages, also signed by _____ (name[s] of other signer[s])."

While fraud-deterrent steps such as these can make it much more difficult for a loose certificate to be removed and misused, there is no absolute protection against its removal and misuse. Notaries must absolutely ensure that while a certificate remains in their control, it is attached only to its intended document.

Do Not Pre-Sign/Seal Certificates. A Notary should never sign and/or seal certificates ahead of time or permit other persons to attach loose notarial certificates to documents. Nor should the Notary send an unattached, signed, and sealed loose certificate through the mail — blank or completed — even if requested to do so by a signer who previously appeared before the Notary. These actions are prohibited by Florida law because they may facilitate fraud or forgery, and they could subject the Notary to lawsuits to recover damages resulting from the Notary's neglect or misconduct (FS 117.107[3]).

Correcting Certificates. A Notary may not change anything in a Notary certificate after the notarization is complete. State officials consider a notarization "complete" after the signer leaves the presence of the Notary after having a document notarized (FS 117.107[7-8]).

If a document and the incorrect — or incomplete — certificate are returned to the Notary, the Notary should treat the transaction as a new notarization; the signer must again personally appear and be identified by the Notary. A note should be made on the original notarial certificate saying that the document has been renotarized due to an error in the original certificate. Likewise, the new notarial certificate should have a notation stating the same.

For additional information or for questions regarding specific situations, contact the Governor's Notary Section at (850) 922-6400.

False Certificate. A Notary who knowingly completes a false notarial certificate is guilty of a felony of the third degree and subject to criminal penalties. A Notary would be completing a false certificate, for example, if he or she signed and sealed an acknowledgment certificate indicating that a signer personally appeared when the signer actually did not (FS 117.105).

Notary Seal

Requirement. A Florida Notary must affix an impression of an official seal on the certificate portion of every document notarized (FS 117.05[3]).

Inking Seal. For paper documents, the official seal of office is a rubber stamp inking seal. The seal must imprint a photographically reproducible impression in black ink (FS 117.05[3][a]).

An embosser may be used *in addition* to the required photographically reproducible seal, but not in place of it. The embosser must not be used over the ink seal or over the Notary's signature (FS 117.05[3][a]).

Format. Florida law does not designate a particular size or shape for the official seal. Typical inking seals are rectangular and about one inch wide by two and one-half inches long.

Required Information. The seal impression must clearly show the following information (FS 117.05[3][a]):

• Name of the Notary (exactly as it appears on the commission certificate).

• The words "Notary Public — State of Florida."

• The Notary's commission expiration date.

• The Notary's commission number.

The seal may contain any additional information — such as the name of the Notary's bonding company — or emblems, except for the Great Seal of the State of Florida (2001 RMN, p. 9).

Lost or Misplaced Seal. A Notary whose seal is lost, misplaced or believed to be in someone else's possession, must immediately notify the Department of State or the Governor in writing (FS 117.05[3][d]).

Possession of Seal. Any person who unlawfully possesses a Notary Public's seal or any papers relating to notarial acts is guilty of a misdemeanor of the second degree (FS 117.05[3][e]).

Placement of Seal Impression. The Notary's official seal impression should be placed near his or her signature on the notarial certificate. It must be easily readable and should not be placed over signatures or any printed matter on the document. An illegible or improperly placed seal may result in rejection of the document by a recorder (FS 117.05[4][i]).

L.S. The letters "L.S." — from the Latin locus sigilli, meaning "location of the seal" — appear on many notarial certificates to indicate where the Notary seal should be placed. Only an embosser seal, used optionally in addition to an inking seal, should be placed over these letters. The inking seal should be placed near but not over the letters.

Fees for Notarial Services

Maximum Fees. The following maximum fees for performing notarial acts are allowed by Florida law (FS 28.24[29], 117.045 and 117.05[2]):

- Acknowledgments — $10. For taking an acknowledgment, the fee is not to exceed $10 for each certificate. For notarizing a document with three signatures, a maximum of $10 may be charged. However, if three certificates are used for the same notarization, then $30 may be charged.

- Certified Copy — $10. A maximum of $10 per copy may be charged by a Notary for providing a certified copy.

- Taking Inventory of a Safe-Deposit Box — $10. For being present at the opening of a safe-deposit box and completing the certificate, the maximum fee is $10.

- Jurats — $10. For executing a jurat, including the administration of the oath or affirmation, the fee is not to exceed $10 per certificate.

- Marriages — $30. For solemnizing the rites of matrimony, the Notary may not charge more than $30.

- Oaths and Affirmations — $10. For administering an oath or affirmation, with or without completion of a jurat, the fee is not to exceed $10 per person.

- Verifying a Vehicle Identification Number — $20. Since the VIN and Odometer Verification form requires the Notary to perform two separate notarial acts, a sum of $20 may be charged — $10 for executing the jurat on Part A and $10 for completing Part B.

Option Not to Charge. Notaries are not required to charge for their notarial services, and they may charge any fee less than the maximum.

Overcharging. Charging more than the legally prescribed fees is reason for the Governor to suspend a Notary's commission (FS 117.01[4][i]).

Travel Fees. Charges for travel by a Notary are not specified by law. Such fees should be charged only if the Notary and signer agree beforehand on the amount to be charged. The signer should understand that a travel fee is not stipulated by law and is a private arrangement separate from the authorized notarial fees described above.

Absentee Ballots. A Notary may not charge a fee for witnessing an absentee ballot in an election, but must witness the ballot if so requested by a voter (FS 117.05[2][b]).

Incomplete Documents

Do Not Notarize. Florida Notaries are specifically prohibited from notarizing a signature on a document that is incomplete (FS 117.107[10]).

Any blanks in a document should be filled in by the signer. If the blanks are inapplicable and intended to be left unfilled, the signer should be asked to line through each space (using ink) or to write "Not Applicable" or "N/A."

An endorsement or assignment in blank of a negotiable or nonnegotiable note and the assignment in blank of any instrument given as security for such note is not considered incomplete.

Notaries are also specifically prohibited from signing and sealing blank notarial certificates and trusting another person to fill them out (FS 117.107[3]).

Disqualifying Interest

Impartiality. Notaries are appointed by the state to be impartial, disinterested witnesses whose screening duties help ensure the integrity of important legal and commercial transactions. Lack of impartiality by a Notary throws doubt on the integrity and lawfulness of any transaction. A Notary must never notarize his or her own signature, or notarize in a transaction in which the Notary has a financial or beneficial interest (FS 117.107[12]).

Financial or Beneficial Interest. A Notary should not perform any notarization related to a transaction in which that Notary has a direct financial or beneficial interest (FS 117.107[12]).

A financial or beneficial interest exists when the Notary is individually named as a principal or beneficiary in a financial transaction or when the Notary receives an advantage, right, privilege, property or fee valued in excess of the lawfully prescribed notarial fee.

Exceptions. A Notary who notarizes for an employer that receives a benefit from a transaction is not considered to have a disqualifying interest unless he or she receives a benefit other than his or her salary and the statutory fee for notarization. In addition, a Notary who is an attorney does not have a disqualifying interest in notarizing the signature of a client unless he or she is a party to or named in the document (FS 117.107[12]).

Any challenged case of disqualifying financial or beneficial interest would be decided in court on its own merits. Thus, it is always safest for a Notary to have no financial or beneficial interest whatsoever in a transaction regardless of what the law allows.

Refusal of Services

Legal Request for Services. Ideally, as officers appointed to serve the general public, Notaries should honor all lawful and reasonable requests to notarize, regardless of the signer's client or nonclient status and without discrimination or personal bias.

However, the Governor's Notary Section has opined that it is not unlawful discrimination for an employee-Notary to limit service to the customers of a Notary's employer or to transactions that are solely related to the business purposes of the Notary's employer during the Notary's normal working hours (2001 RMN, p. 56).

Reasonable Care

Responsibility. As public servants, Notaries must act responsibly and exercise reasonable care in the performance of their official duties. If a Notary fails to do so, he or she may be subject to a civil suit to recover financial damages caused by the Notary's error or omission. In general, reasonable care is that degree of concern and attentiveness that a person of normal intelligence and responsibility would exhibit. If a Notary can show a judge or jury that he or she did everything expected of a reasonable person, the judge or jury is obligated by law to find the Notary not liable for damages.

Complying with all pertinent laws is the first rule of reasonable care for a Notary. If there are no statutory guidelines in a given instance, the Notary should "bend over backwards" to use common sense and prudence. (See "Steps to Proper Notarization," pages 12–15.)

Unauthorized Practice of Law

<u>Do Not Assist Others with Legal Matters</u>. A nonattorney Notary may not give legal advice or accept fees for legal advice. The nonattorney Notary may not assist a signer in drafting, preparing, selecting, completing or understanding a document or transaction.

The Notary should not fill in blank spaces in the text of a document for other persons, tell others what documents they need or how to draft them, or advise others about the legal sufficiency of a document — and especially not for a fee.

A Notary may fill in the blanks on the portion of any document containing the notarial certificate. And a Notary, as a private individual, may prepare legal documents that he or she is personally a party to, but the Notary may not then notarize his or her signature on these same documents.

Notaries who overstep their authority by advising others on legal matters have committed a felony of the third degree (FS 454.23).

<u>Exceptions</u>. Nonattorney Notaries certified or licensed in a particular field (e.g., real estate, insurance or escrow) may offer advice in that field. Paralegals under the supervision of an attorney may advise others about documents in routine legal matters.

Signature by Mark

<u>Mark Serves as Signature</u>. A person who cannot sign his or her name because of illiteracy or disability may instead use a mark — an "X" for example — as a signature, as long as there are two witnesses to the making of the mark (FS 117.05[14][b]).

<u>Witnesses</u>. In order for a mark to be acknowledged or sworn to before a Notary, two witnesses should sign the document (e.g., "John Q. Smith, Witness") and the Notary's journal. The Notary should print legibly the marker's name beside the mark on the document in the following manner (FS 117.05[14][b]):

John   X   Doe
His Mark

<u>Signature by Mark Certificate</u>. A mark is generally considered

a signature under law, as long as it is properly witnessed. Florida law provides special notarial certificates for persons signing by mark (FS 117.05[14][c]):

• For an Acknowledgment in an Individual Capacity:

_____ First Name _____ Last Name
_____ His or Her Mark

State of Florida
County of _____

The foregoing instrument was acknowledged before me this _____ day of _____ (month), _____ (year), by _____ (name of person), who signed with a mark in the presence of these witnesses: _____ (Names of witnesses).

_____ (Signature of Notary)   (Seal of Notary)

_____ (Name of Notary, printed, typed or stamped)

Personally known _____ OR produced identification _____

Type of identification produced _____

• For an Oath or Affirmation:

_____ First Name _____ Last Name
_____ His or Her Mark

State of Florida
County of _____

Sworn to (or affirmed) and subscribed before me this _____ day of _____ (month), _____ (year), by _____ (name of person making statement), who signed with a mark in the presence of these witnesses: _____ (Names of witnesses).

_____ (Signature of Notary)   (Seal of Notary)

_____ (Name of Notary, printed, typed or stamped)

Personally known _____ OR produced identification _____

Type of identification produced _____

Notarizing for One Who Directs the Notary to Sign

Persons with a Disability. If a person cannot sign a document due to a physical disability, he or she may direct the Notary to sign on his or her behalf (FS 117.05[14][d]).

Procedure. The person with the disability must be in the presence of the Notary when directing the Notary to sign a document on his or her behalf. The Notary must then sign the document in the presence of two impartial witnesses.

After signing the name of the person, the Notary must write below the signature the following statement: "Signature affixed by Notary pursuant to Section 117.05(14), Florida Statutes," and also state in the notarial certificate the circumstances of the signing (FS 117.05[14][d]).

Notarization. A Notary may then notarize this signature but should take extra care to avoid any problems. As with any notarization, the Notary must determine the signer's willingness to sign and whether or not the signer understands the purpose of the document.

Identification of Principal. The Notary must positively identify the principal — the person directing the Notary to sign — through personal knowledge, credible identifying witness(es) or ID cards.

Certificates. The following certificates are set out by Florida law for performing a notarization for a person with a disability who directs the Notary to sign on his or her behalf (FS 117.05[14][e]):

• For an Acknowledgment in an Individual Capacity:

State of Florida
County of _____

The foregoing instrument was acknowledged before me this _____ day of _____ (month), _____ (year), by _____ (name of person acknowledging), and subscribed by _____ (name of Notary) at the direction of and in the presence of _____ (name of person acknowledging), and in the presence of these witnesses: _____ (Names of witnesses).

_____ (Signature of Notary)   (Seal of Notary)
_____ (Name of Notary, printed, typed or stamped)
Personally known _____ OR produced identification _____
Type of identification produced _____

• For an Oath or Affirmation:

State of Florida

County of _____

Sworn to (or affirmed) before me this _____ day of _____ (month), _____ (year), by _____ (name of person making statement), and subscribed by _____ (name of Notary) at the direction of and in the presence of _____ (name of person making statement), and in the presence of these witnesses: _____ (Names of witnesses).

_____ (Signature of Notary)   (Seal of Notary)

_____ (Name of Notary, printed, typed or stamped)

Personally known _____ OR produced identification _____

Type of identification produced _____

Journal Entry. The prudent Notary will record the specific circumstances of the notarization in a journal and ask all persons involved to sign the journal as well.

Notarizing for the Blind

Read Document. A Notary may not notarize for a blind person without first reading the document to the person. The reading should be verbatim. However, to avoid the unauthorized practice of law, the Notary must not attempt to explain the document (FS 117.05[14][a]).

Notarizing for Minors

Under Age 18. Generally, persons must reach the age of majority before they can handle their own legal affairs and sign documents for themselves. In Florida, the age of majority is 18. Normally, parents or guardians will sign on a minor's behalf. In certain cases, where minors are engaged in business transactions or serving as court witnesses, they may lawfully sign documents and have their signatures notarized.

Include Age Next to Signature. When notarizing for a minor, the Notary should ask the young signer to write his or her age next to the signature to alert any person relying upon the document that the signer is a minor. The Notary is not required to verify the minor signer's age.

Identification. The method for identifying a minor is the same as that for an adult. However, because minors often do not possess acceptable identification documents, such as driver's licenses or passports, determining the identity of a minor can be a problem.

In Florida, anyone 12 years of age or older may be issued a state non-driver's ID, which the Notary may use as identification.

If the minor does not have an acceptable ID, then the other methods of identifying acknowledgers must be used: either the Notary's personal knowledge of the minor or the oath of a credible identifying witness or witnesses who can identify the minor. (See "Credible Identifying Witness[es]," pages 40–42.)

Authentication

Documents Sent Out of State. Documents notarized in Florida and sent to other states may be required to bear proof that the Notary's signature and seal are genuine and that the Notary had authority to act at the time of notarization. This process of proving the genuineness of an official signature and seal is called authentication or legalization.

In Florida, the proof is in the form of an authenticating certificate attached to the notarized document by the Department of State. These certificates are known by different names: certificates of authority, certificates of capacity, certificates of authenticity, certificates of prothonotary and "flags."

An authenticating certificate from the Florida Secretary of State costs $10. It is not the Notary's responsibility to pick up or pay for the certificate of authority. To obtain a certificate of authority, the document signer must submit by mail a written request with the notarized document, a self-addressed, stamped envelope if the document is to be returned by mail, and a check or money order payable to "Department of State" to (FS 117.103):

Department of State
Division of Corporations
Apostille Certification
P.O. Box 6800
Tallahassee, FL 32314-6800
(850) 245-6945

Documents Sent Out of Country. If the notarized document is going outside the United States, a chain authentication process may be necessary and additional certificates of authority may have to be obtained from the U.S. Department of State in Washington, D.C., a foreign embassy in Washington, D.C. and a ministry of foreign affairs in the particular foreign nation.

Apostilles and the Hague Convention. Fortunately, over 90 nations, including the United States, subscribe to a treaty that simplifies authentication of notarized documents exchanged between any of the nations. The official name of this treaty, adopted by the Conference on October 5, 1961, is the *Hague Convention Abolishing the Requirement of Legalization for Foreign Public Documents* (for a list of the subscribing countries, see "Hague Convention Nations," pages 122–124).

Under the Hague Convention, only one authenticating certificate, called an apostille, is necessary to ensure acceptance of a Notary's signature and stamp in these subscribing countries. (Apostille means "notation" in French.)

Apostilles are issued by the Florida Department of State. The procedure and fee are the same as for obtaining an authenticating certificate. To assist the department in determining the correct type of authenticating certificate, any request must include the country of destination.

Advertising

False or Misleading Advertising. A Notary's commission can be suspended if the Notary uses false or misleading advertising to misrepresent the authority, rights and privileges of a Notary. For example, a Notary who represents himself or herself to be an immigration expert and who leads clients to believe that he or she has powers beyond that of a Florida Notary is guilty of false advertising (FS 117.01[4][e]).

Foreign-Language Advertising. A nonattorney Notary advertising notarial services in a foreign language must take steps to guard against misinterpretation of his or her authorized function. Notaries are required to include in any such foreign-language advertisement the following statement in English and in the foreign language (FS 117.05[10]):

I AM NOT AN ATTORNEY LICENSED TO PRACTICE LAW IN THE STATE OF FLORIDA, AND I MAY NOT GIVE LEGAL ADVICE OR ACCEPT FEES FOR LEGAL ADVICE.

The statement must be shown in a conspicuous size and applies to signs and all other forms of written communication (e.g., business cards, printed ads) with the exception of a single desk plaque. If the ad is by radio or television, this statement may be modified but must contain the same information (FS 117.05[10]).

Translation of 'Notary Public.' Literal translation of "Notary Public" into a language other than English (e.g. in Spanish, *Notario Publico* or *Notaria Publica*) is prohibited by law (FS 117.05[11]).

Foreign Languages

Foreign-Language Documents. Florida Notaries are not expressly prohibited from notarizing non-English documents. As long as the notarial certificate and document signature are in English or in a language the Notary can read, Florida Notaries may notarize foreign-language documents.

However, there are difficulties to consider with foreign-language documents: blatant fraud might go undetected; the U.S. Notary seal might be misinterpreted in another country; and making a journal entry might be difficult.

Foreign-Language Signers. There should always be direct communication between the Notary and document signer — whether in English or any other language. The Notary should never rely upon an intermediary or interpreter to be assured that a signer is willing, aware and understands the transaction, because this third party may have a motive for misrepresenting the circumstances to the Notary and/or to the signer.

Specifically, Florida law prohibits a Notary from notarizing for a signer who does not speak or understand the English language unless the nature and effect of the document is translated into a language that the signer understands (FS 117.107[6]).

Immigration

Documents. Certain immigration documents may be notarized, including the I-134/I-864, also known as the Affidavit of Support. However, federal law (see "Naturalization Certificates," below) does pose certain restrictions on the Notary in the area of immigration.

Naturalization Certificates. A Notary may only photocopy a certificate of naturalization for lawful purposes. The NNA recommends that a Notary only certify a copy of the certificate if written directions are provided by a U.S. immigration authority.

Military Officer Notarizations

May Notarize Worldwide. Certain U.S. military officers may notarize for military personnel and their dependents anywhere in the world. Under statutory authority, the following persons are authorized to act as Notaries:

- Civilian attorneys employed as legal assistance attorneys and licensed to practice law in the United States.

- Judge advocates on active duty or training as reservists on inactive duty.

- All adjutants, assistant adjutants, acting adjutants and personnel adjutants.

- Enlisted paralegals, personnel rank E-4 or higher, on active duty or training on inactive duty.

- Active duty personnel who are commissioned officers or senior noncommissioned officers (rank E-7 or higher) who are stationed at a Geographically Separated Unit (GSU) or location where no authorized Notary official is available, and who are appointed in writing by the unit's servicing general court-martial convening authority.

Certificate. When signing documents in an official capacity, military-officer Notaries must specify the date and location of the notarization, list their title and office and use a raised seal or inked stamp citing Title 10 U.S.C. 1044a (U.S. Code, Title 10, Sections 936, 1044a).

Florida law provides the following wording (FS 695.031[2]):

On this _____ day of _____ (month), _____ (year), before me _____ (name of officer taking acknowledgment), the undersigned officer, personally appeared _____ (name of person acknowledging), known to me (or satisfactorily proven) to be serving in or with, or whose duties require his or her presence with the Armed Forces of the United States, and to be the person whose name is subscribed to the within instrument, and acknowledged that he or she executed the same for the purposes therein contained, and the undersigned does further certify that he or she is at the date of this certificate a commissioned officer of the rank stated below and is in the active service of the Armed Forces of the United States.

_____ (Signature of commissioned officer)

_____ (Rank of commissioned officer and command or branch of service to which officer is attached)

Wills

Do Not Offer Advice. Often, people attempt to draw up wills without benefit of legal counsel and then bring these homemade testaments to a Notary to have them "legalized," expecting the Notary to know how to proceed. In advising or assisting such persons, the Notary risks prosecution for the unauthorized practice of law; the Notary's ill-informed advice may do considerable damage to the affairs of the signer (2001 RMN, p. 60).

Wills are highly sensitive documents, the format of which is dictated by strict laws. The slightest deviation from these laws can nullify a will. In some cases, holographic (handwritten) wills have actually been voided by notarization.

Authority. A Florida Notary may notarize a will, whether prepared by an attorney or not, provided the following conditions are met (2001 RMN, p. 60):

- The document signer is present and appears to understand the purpose of the document.

- The signer is personally known or is able to produce acceptable identification. The signer may not be identified by credible witness(es).

- The document contains preprinted jurat wording, or the signer directs the Notary to provide a type of notarization.

Self-Proving Wills. Typically, self-proving wills shorten and simplify the probate process. A will or codicil (amendment to a will) may be self-proved before a Notary at the time of its execution with the acknowledgment of the testator and affidavits of two witnesses. The Notary should complete a certificate in substantially the following form (FS 732.503):

State of Florida

County of _____

We, _____, _____ and _____, the testator and the witnesses, respectively, whose names are signed to the attached or foregoing instrument, having been sworn, declared to the undersigned officer that the testator, in the presence of witnesses, signed the instrument as the testator's last will (codicil), that the testator (signed) (or directed another to sign for him or her), and that each of the witnesses, in the presence of the testator and in the presence of each other, signed the will as a witness.

_____ (Signature of testator)

_____ (Signature of witness)

_____ (Signature of witness)

Subscribed and sworn to before me by _____, the testator who is personally known to me or who has produced _____ (type of identification) as identification, and by _____ a witness who is personally known to me or who has produced _____ (type of identification) as identification, and by _____, a witness who is personally known to me or who has produced _____ (type of identification) as identification, on _____ (month/day), _____ (year).

_____ (Signature of Notary)   (Seal of Notary)

_____ (Name of Notary, printed, typed or stamped)

<u>Witnesses</u>. Florida law provides that any competent person may act as a witness to a will. Ideally, the witness should be impartial and have no financial or beneficial interest in the person's estate or the document being presented (FS 732.504).

<u>Living Wills</u>. Documents that are popularly called "living wills" may be notarized. These are not actually wills at all, but written statements of the signer's wishes concerning medical treatment in the event that the person has an illness or injury and is unable to issue instructions on his or her own behalf.

Affidavits

<u>Purpose</u>. An affidavit is a signed statement made under oath or affirmation by a person called an affiant, and it is used for a variety of purposes, both in and out of court.

Affidavits are used to make sworn statements for many reasons, from declaring losses to an insurance company to declaring U.S. citizenship before traveling to a foreign country. An affidavit is a document containing a statement voluntarily signed and sworn to or affirmed before a Notary or other official with oath-administering powers. If used in a judicial proceeding, only one side in the case need participate in the affidavit process, in contrast to the deposition.

Procedure. For an affidavit, the Notary must administer an oath or affirmation and complete some form of jurat, which the Notary signs and seals.

In an affidavit, the Notary's certificate typically sandwiches the affiant's signed statement, with the venue and affiant's name at the top of the document and the jurat wording at the end. The Notary is responsible for the venue, affiant's name and any notarial text at the beginning and end of the affidavit. The affiant is responsible for the signed statement in the middle.

Certificate for Affidavits. Affidavits typically require jurat certificates. (See "Jurats," pages 31–32.)

Oath (Affirmation) for Affidavits. If no other wording is prescribed, a Notary may use the following language in administering an oath (affirmation) for an affidavit or deposition:

> Do you solemnly swear that the statements made in this affidavit are the truth, the whole truth, and nothing but the truth, so help you God?

> (Do you solemnly affirm that the statements made in this affidavit are the truth, the whole truth, and nothing but the truth?)

Response Required. For an oath or affirmation, the affiant must respond aloud and affirmatively, with "I do," "Yes" or the like.

Depositions

Purpose. A deposition is a signed transcript of the signer's oral statements taken down for use in a judicial proceeding. This deposition signer is called the deponent.

With a deposition, both sides in a lawsuit or court case have the opportunity to cross-examine the deponent. Questions and answers are transcribed into a written statement. Used only in judicial proceedings, a deposition is then signed and sworn to before an oath-administering official.

Procedure. Florida Notaries who are not licensed attorneys do not have the power to take depositions. This duty is most often executed by trained and certified shorthand reporters, also known as court reporters. Notaries may administer the oath or affirmation to the deponent only (2001 RMN, pp. 13–14).

For a deposition, the Notary typically administers an oath or affirmation and completes some form of jurat, which he or she signs and seals.

Certificate for Depositions. To administer an oath or affirmation to the deponent, the Notary uses a jurat certificate. *The Governor's Reference Manual for Notaries* prescribes the following certificate (2001 RMN, p. 14):

State of Florida

County of _____

In my capacity as a Notary Public of the State of Florida, I certify that on the _____ day of _____ (month), _____ (year), at _____ (time) a.m./p.m., _____ (name of deponent) personally appeared before me and took an oath (or affirmation) for the purpose of giving testimony in the matter: _____.

_____ (Signature of Notary)   (Seal of Notary)

_____ (Name of Notary, printed, typed or stamped)

Personally known _____ OR produced identification _____

Type of identification produced _____

Oath (Affirmation) for Depositions. If no other wording is prescribed, a Notary may use the following language in administering an oath (affirmation) for an affidavit or deposition:

Do you solemnly swear that the statements made in this deposition are the truth, the whole truth and nothing but the truth, so help you God?

(Do you solemnly affirm that the statements made in this deposition are the truth, the whole truth and nothing but the truth?)

Response Required. For an oath or affirmation, the affiant must respond aloud and affirmatively, with "I do," "Yes" or the like.

MISCONDUCT, FINES AND PENALTIES

Maintenance of Commission

Application Misstatement. Significant misstatement or omission in the application for a Notary commission is reason for the Governor to suspend a Notary's commission (FS 117.01[4][a]).

Commission Name. A person may not apply for a Notary commission in a name other than his or her legal name. A person applying for a commission must submit proof of identity to the Department of State upon request. A person who violates this provision is guilty of a felony of the third degree (FS 117.05[1]).

Falsely Acting as a Notary. Any person who willfully acts as a Notary while not lawfully commissioned is guilty of a misdemeanor in the second degree. Also guilty is a Notary who knowingly acts as such after his or her commission has expired (FS 117.05[7] and [8]).

Failure to Report Name or Address Change. A Notary who fails to report a change of name, address or telephone number is guilty of neglect of duty, and his or her commission may be suspended. This includes failure to request an amended commission after making such change (FS 117.01[4][g] and 117.05[9]).

Failure to Maintain Bond. Failure to maintain the required $7,500 bond as prescribed in the law is cause for the Governor to suspend the Notary's commission (FS 117.01[4][j]). (See "Notary Bond," pages 17–18.)

Commission Suspension. If the Notary receives notice from the Department of State that his or her office has been declared vacant or the commission has been suspended, the Notary shall immediately mail or deliver the commission to the Secretary of State and destroy the official Notary seal (FS 117.01[5]).

Illegal and Improper Acts

Official Misconduct. Commission of an act involving dishonesty, fraud or intentional violation of any notarial law is reason for the Governor to refuse to grant, revoke or suspend a Notary's commission (FS 117.01[4][d]).

Official misconduct comprises intent to benefit oneself or to cause harm to another, including knowingly falsifying or causing someone to falsify a document. Official misconduct is a felony in the third degree (FS 838.022).

Notarization Without Appearance. Notarizing the signature of a person who does not personally appear before the Notary at the time of notarization is an act of official misconduct. A Notary who violates the law regarding personal appearance is guilty of a civil infraction and can be fined up to $5,000, even if the Notary had no fraudulent intentions. A violator with intent to defraud is guilty of felony in the third degree (FS 117.107[9]).

Notary's Own Signature. Notaries are not permitted to notarize their own signatures (FS 117.05[1]).

Beneficial Interest. A Notary Public may not notarize a document in which his or her name appears as a party to the transaction (FS 117.107[12]).

Notarizing for Relatives. The law specifically prohibits a Notary from notarizing for a spouse, son, daughter, mother or father of the Notary (FS 117.107[11]).

Mentally Incapacitated. If the Notary knows that the document signer has been judged mentally incapacitated and the notarization requires exercise of rights that have been removed pursuant to Florida Statutes, Section 744.3215(2) or (3), the Notary may not notarize (FS 117.107[4]).

Certifying Copies of Recordable Documents. A Notary is not authorized to certify a copy of a document that is a public record if a copy can be made by another public official (FS 117.05[12][a]).
A Notary also may not certify a document that is a vital record in Florida or any state or U.S. territory (FS 117.05[12]).

Incomplete Documents. It is unlawful for a Florida Notary to notarize a document that is not complete. This prohibition does not apply to a negotiable or nonnegotiable note, or to a document given as security for such a note (FS 117.107[10]).

Blank Certificates. A Notary may not sign and affix a seal to a blank notarial certificate and then deliver that certificate to another person for the purpose of notarization (FS 117.107[3]).

False Certificate. A Notary who knowingly completes a false notarial certificate or who falsely or fraudulently takes an acknowledgment is guilty of a felony in the third degree, which is punishable by a $5,000 fine or up to five years in jail. A Notary completes a false certificate, for example, if he or she signed and sealed an acknowledgment certificate indicating that a signer personally appeared when the signer actually did not (FS 117.105).

Signing False Names. A Notary may not sign a notarial certificate using any other name than the one under which he or she was commissioned (FS 117.107[1]).

Unlawful Possession. Any person who unlawfully possesses a Notary seal or any papers relating to notarial acts is guilty of a misdemeanor in the second degree. Such conviction is punishable by a fine of $500 or up to 60 days in jail (FS 117.05[3][e]).

False or Misleading Advertising. The use of false or misleading advertising by a Notary to represent that he or she has duties, rights and privileges not given by law is grounds for the Governor to suspend a Notary's commission (FS 117.01[4][e]).

This includes failing to include in a foreign language advertisement the statement, "I am not an attorney licensed to practice law in the state of Florida, and I may not give legal advice or accept fees for legal advice," or including a literal translation of the words "Notary Public" into a language other than English (FS 117.05[10] and [11]). (See "Advertising," pages 57–58.)

Unauthorized Practice of Law. The unauthorized practice of law, such as giving advice about a legal document when one is not a lawyer, is reason for the Governor to suspend a Notary's commission (FS 117.01[4][f]).

A Notary is not authorized to change anything in a written instrument after it has been signed by anyone (FS 117.107[7]).

It is also considered the unauthorized practice of law for a Notary to take a deposition. Notaries may only administer an oath or affirmation to a deponent (FS 454.23).

Overcharging. Charging more than the legally prescribed fees is reason for the Governor to refuse to grant or to suspend a Notary's commission (FS 117.01[4][i]).

Misrepresentation. Commission of an act involving misrepresentation of authority or commission of fraud comprises neglect of duty and is grounds for suspension of the Notary's commission by the Governor (FS 117.01[4][h]).

Acknowledgment in Lieu of Oath. A Notary may not take an acknowledgment in lieu of an oath if an oath is required (FS 117.03).

Must Identify Signer. A Notary may not notarize a signature on a document unless the Notary personally knows, or has satisfactory evidence that the person is the one described in the document (FS 117.05[5]).

Facsimile of Notary's Signature. A Notary may not use a facsimile stamp to affix his or her official signature unless the Notary has a physical disability that limits his or her ability to sign his or her name. The Notary must submit written notice to the Department of State, along with a sample of the facsimile signature stamp (FS 117.107[2]).

Signer Doesn't Understand. A Notary may not notarize a document if it appears that the signer is mentally incapable of understanding the nature and significance of the document at the time of notarization (FS 117.107[5]).

Foreign-Language Documents and Signers. A Notary may not take the acknowledgment of a person who does not speak or understand the English language, unless the nature of the document to be notarized is translated into a language that the signer can understand (FS 117.107[6]).

Correcting Certificates. A Notary may not change anything in a notarial certificate once the notarization is complete. State officials consider a notarization "complete" when the signer leaves the presence of the Notary after having a document notarized (FS 117.107[8]). (See "Correcting Certificates," page 47.)

Seal Exclusive Property. The official notarial seal is the exclusive property of the Notary named on it. An employer may not retain the Notary's seal after termination of the Notary's employment. Any person who unlawfully possesses a Notary's seal is guilty of a misdemeanor of the second degree (FS 117.05[3] [c] and [e]).

Liability and Investigation

Liability for Damages. A Notary and the surety company bonding the Notary may be sued by any person who has been damaged by the Notary's official acts. The surety is liable only up to the amount of the bond, which is $7,500 in Florida, but a Notary may be found liable for any amount of money (FS 117.01[7]).

Employer Liability. If a Notary's official misconduct causes any individual to be financially damaged, then the Notary's employer may be liable to the person for all damages if the Notary was acting within the scope of his or her employment at the time that he or she engaged in the misconduct (FS 117.05[6]).

Complaint and Investigation. A Notary's commission can be suspended or denied for any complaint found to have merit by the Governor. Failure to cooperate or respond to an investigation by the Governor's office regarding such a complaint is also cause for commission suspension or denial.

ELECTRONIC NOTARIZATION

Electronic commerce produces a need for Notaries to witness electronic transactions, just as Notaries have witnessed paper transactions for centuries. While the tools for creating and signing documents may be different, the impartial witnessing services of a Notary remain the same and are as important as ever.

Legislative Enactments. In June 2000, the U.S. Congress enacted the Electronic Signatures in Global and National Commerce Act. Commonly known as E-Sign, the act provides nationwide authorization for the use of electronic signatures and notarizations. E-Sign is the governing electronic transactions law unless a state formally enacts the Uniform Electronic Transactions Act (UETA) as published by the National Conference of Commissioners on Uniform State Laws.

Florida enacted the UETA in 2000. UETA is a set of model laws designed to provide uniform standards for states enacting legislation for the use and acceptance of electronic transactions. Like E-Sign, UETA authorizes Notaries to electronically sign and notarize signatures on paperless documents.

Effective June 2007, Florida enacted the Uniform Real Property Electronic Recording Act (URPERA), which enables county recorders to accept electronic documents for recordation in the land records.

Also in 2007, the Florida Legislature enacted amendments to Chapter 117 — codified in Section117.021 of the Florida Statutes — authorizing Notaries to perform electronic notarizations, prescribing performance standards for a Notary's electronic signature, clarifying that an image of an official Notary seal is not required in an electronic notarization if the Notary's electronic signature includes certain information found in the seal and authorizing the Department of State to publish administrative rules to ensure the security, reliability and uniformity of electronic signatures and seals.

Administrative Rules Promulgated. On January 6, 2010 the Department of State issued final electronic notarization rules as an amendment to the Florida Administrative Code Section Chapter 1N-5.

Key Terms and Concepts

Electronic Record or Document. Under the UETA, an "electronic record" is information that is stored in an electronic or other medium and is retrievable in perceivable form. For example, a computer word processing file would be considered an electronic record under this definition.

Under the URPERA, an "electronic document" is a document that is stored in an electronic or other medium and retrievable or received by a county recorder in an electronic form (FS 695.27[2] [a] and [c]). Essentially, an electronic record and document are one and the same, but in the URPERA "document" was preferred over "record" because "record" has a specific meaning in real property recording law.

Electronic Signature. A paper document is signed with pen and ink, but an electronic document — one that is created, sent, received or stored by electronic means — may be "signed" and authenticated with an electronic signature using any available technology. Florida law defines an electronic signature as an electronic sound, symbol or process executed by a person with the intent to sign an electronic document and is attached to or logically associated with a document such that, when recorded, it is assigned the same document number or a consecutive page number immediately following such document (FS 668.50 [2][h], 695.27 [2][d]).

Examples of electronic signatures may include:

- a typed name, such as one on the signature line of an electronic document or at the bottom of an email;

- a "click wrap" signature created when a signer clicks an "I accept" or "Click to Sign" option in a software application, in an electronic form or on a Web site, such as when purchasing items online with a credit card;

- a scanned digitalized image of a handwritten signature pasted into an electronic document;

- a "holographic" signature affixed by hand on a digitalized signing pad or device, such as those currently used by major retail stores, UPS and FedEx;

- a "voice print," based on the unique physical configuration of the speaker's mouth and throat, which expresses the vocal sample as a mathematical formula;

- a "sound," such as a voice message left by telephone;

- a Personal Identification Number (PIN), such as those used at a bank ATM to obtain cash;

- a telephone signature, using the dial pad of a touch-tone phone to navigate a prompt system to accept terms of an agreement;

- a "digital" signature affixed by applying cryptographic methods (See "Public Key Certificate" and "Digital Signature," pages 72–73).

Technological Neutrality. A cardinal tenet of the UETA is "technological neutrality." It does not require, specify or endorse a particular technology for creating, signing, transmitting and storing electronic signatures. Instead, the parties involved in a transaction must agree upon the technology used to sign a document electronically.

Intent. One of the most important legal considerations of any electronic signature is intent. Regardless of the actual technology used to create an e-signature, the party using the technology must adopt it with the intent to sign the electronic document. In other words, any technology may be used as an electronic signature as long as the e-signature expresses the signer's intent to sign the electronic document.

Attribution and Security Procedure. Another critically important legal consideration of any electronic signature is attribution. In legal language, the term "attribution" is used to describe the process of determining that a signature is the act of a given person (FS 695.27[2][d]). Attribution of electronic signatures can pose special problems because the signatories may not be present at the time of signing.

UETA allows parties executing an e-signed electronic record to use a "security procedure" to determine the identity of the person to whom the electronic signature is attributable. Such a procedure can detect any changes or errors in the electronic record or signature as well. A security procedure can use technological means — including algorithms or other codes, identifying words or numbers, encryption, callback or other acknowledgment procedures, and the like — to prove that a signature is the act of a given person and that the content of the document has been changed since it was signed (FS 117.021[2]).

Since "acknowledgment procedures" is left intentionally broad by the UETA, the witnessing act of a Notary Public in an electronic notarization qualifies as a security procedure for proving the attribution of an electronic signature and informational integrity of an electronic record.

The Florida Administrative Code requires that the Notary's electronic signature must be attributable to the Notary (FAC 1N-5.001[7], [8]) and 5.002[1]).

Notary's Electronic Signature. In performing an electronic notarial act, a Notary Public must use an electronic signature that meets four important performance standards (FS 117.021[2] and FAC 1N-5.001).

- It must be unique to the Notary: the signature must be attributable to the Notary to the exclusion of all other persons.

- It must be capable of independent verification: the signature must allow any interested person to reasonably determine the Notary's identity and relevant authority, and that the signature is the act of the particular Notary identified by the signature.

- It must be kept under the exclusive control of the Notary: the signature must be accessible by and attributable solely to the Notary to the exclusion of all other persons and entities either through being retained in the direct physical custody of the Notary or secured with one or more biometric, password, token, or other authentication technologies in an electronic notarization system.

- It must be attached to or logically associated with the electronic document in a manner that any subsequent alteration to the electronic document displays evidence of the alteration. That is, the Notary's electronic signature must be securely bound to the electronic document in such a manner as to make it impracticable to falsify or alter, without detection, either the signature or the document.

According to the Florida Administrative Code, a Notary's electronic signature may be affixed by means of an electronic Notary system or public key certificate (FAC 1N-5.002[3] and [4]).

A Notary must use an authentication procedure such as a password, token, card or biometric to protect access to the Notary's electronic signature or the means for affixing the signature (FAC 1N-5.002[2]).

The Notary's electronic signature may contain information from the Notary's official physical seal that may be used in lieu of placing an image of the physical seal on the electronic document. (See "Electronic Seal Information in Lieu of Seal," page 74.)

"Public Key Certificate" and "Digital Signature". A public key certificate is computer software code that utilizes encryption technology, is securely issued to a unique individual and used to create a "digital" signature — a particular type of electronic signature that can provide a recipient with a reason to believe that the message or document was created by a known sender and that it was not altered in transit.

According to the Florida Administrative Code, a public key certificate used to create the Notary's electronic signature must:

- Identify the certification authority issuing it;

- Name or identify its subscriber (user);

- Contain the subscriber's public key; and

- Be digitally signed by the certification authority issuing it (FAC 1N-5.001[9]).

Any public key certificate that is used to affix the Notary's electronic signature and seal information must be issued at the third or higher level of assurance as defined by the U. S. National Institute of Standards and Technology (NIST) Special Publication 800-63 (NIST800-63), Electronic Authentication Guideline Version 1.0.2 (FAC 1N-5.002[5]).

Electronic Notary System. An electronic Notary system is a set of applications, programs, hardware, software or technology designed to enable a Notary to perform electronic notarizations (FAC 1N-5.001[4]). For example, many electronic Notary systems today are accessible over the Internet and run entirely from within a Web browser. Other such systems may be installed on and executed from one's local computer system.

Any electronic Notary system that is used to affix the Notary's electronic signature and seal information must be issued at the third or higher level of assurance as defined by the U. S. National Institute of Standards and Technology (NIST) Special Publication 800-63 (NIST800-63), Electronic Authentication Guideline Version 1.0.2 (FAC 1N-5.002[5]).

Physical Presence Required. Notaries are expressly prohibited from notarizing the physical or electronic signature of any signer who is not in the Notary's presence at the time of notarization (FS 117.021[1] and 107[9]).

Certificate for Electronic Notarization. A notarial act executed by electronic means must be evidenced by a certificate electronically signed and dated by a notarial officer in a manner that attributes the signature to the Notary Public identified on the commission. In addition, the certificate may include the Notary's electronic seal (FS 695.27).

Electronic Seal Information in Lieu of Seal. Notaries do not need to use a physical seal to authenticate an electronic notarization. While a physical seal is not necessary, this does not mean that Notaries do not use a "seal" to indicate their Notary commission and authority. In Florida, a Notary's acknowledgement on an electronic document is considered complete without the imprint of a Notary seal if the following information appears electronically within the message: the Notary's full name as provided on the Notary's application for commission; the words "Notary Public State of Florida"; the commission number and commission expiration date (FS 117.021[3] and FS 695.27[3][c]). ■

Test Your Knowledge

Trial Exam

Instructions. This examination is designed to test your knowledge of the basic concepts of notarization. Work through the exam without looking at the answers, then check your responses and note where you need additional study. Careful review of "Notary Laws Explained" (pages 16–70), the reprinted Notary statutes (pages 77-105), "10 Most-Asked Questions" (pages 7–11) and "Steps to Proper Notarization" (pages 12–15) will produce the answers.

A perfect score on this examination is 100 points. There are:

- 20 true/false questions worth one point each.
- Five multiple-choice questions worth four points each.
- Five fill-in-the-blank questions worth four points each.
- Five essay questions worth eight points each.

Now, get a separate sheet of paper and a pen or pencil, and test your knowledge.

Part 1: True/False. For the following statements, answer true or false. Each correct answer is worth one point:

1. Notaries may act only in the county where they are commissioned. True or false?

2. The maximum Notary fee for completing three acknowledgment certificates is $15. True or false?

3. It is a Notary's duty to serve all persons requesting lawful

notarial acts, even those who are not customers. True or false?

4. Notaries must keep a photocopy of every document notarized. True or false?

5. A deposition is oral testimony that is written down and used as evidence in a court proceeding. True or false?

6. Notaries can withhold their services if they believe a signer is unable to understand a document. True or false?

7. Upon request, it is a Notary's duty to draft powers of attorney, mortgages and deeds. True or false?

8. After the letters "SS." the Notary must write his or her Social Security number. True or false?

9. Holographic wills must be notarized to be valid. True or false?

10. A Notary may rely upon two strangers as credible identifying witnesses as long as both witnesses have acceptable photo IDs. True or false?

11. A Notary can notarize documents which he or she will be signing as a corporate officer. True or false?

12. A Florida Notary may not perform a marriage ceremony for an immediate relative. True or false?

13. The Notary needn't reimburse the surety company for bond funds paid out to a person financially harmed by the Notary's actions. True or false?

14. The letters "L.S." stand for the Latin words locus sigilli, which mean "location of the seal." True or false?

15. A Notary's seal belongs to the Notary's employer if the employer paid for it. True or false?

16. A credible identifying witness vouches for the identity of a signer in the Notary's presence and a subscribing witness

for the genuineness of a signature of a person not in the Notary's presence. True or false?

17. An affirmation is the legal equivalent of an oath, but has no reference to a Supreme Being. True or false?

18. A Notary employed by a corporation may take the acknowledgment of the corporation's president. True or false?

19. Notaries may not refuse to notarize blank or incomplete documents if they are signed in the Notary's presence. True or false?

20. A Notary should not rely upon a third party to interpret the words of a signer who does not speak the Notary's language. True or false?

Multiple Choice. Choose the one best answer to each question. Each correct answer is worth four points.

1. A Notary has no disqualifying interest when acting as …
    a. A cosigner of the document being notarized.
    b. A real estate agent selling the signer a condominium.
    c. A salaried employee of the signer's company.

2. To become a Notary, an applicant must …
    a. Have been a state resident for at least one year.
    b. File a bond and take an oath.
    c. Pass an oral exam given by the Governor's office.

3. A certificate of authority for a Notary may be obtained …
    a. From the Governor's office or the county clerk.
    b. From a stationery store or the Notary himself/herself.
    c. From the Florida Department of State.

4. "Satisfactory evidence" of identity means reliance upon …
    a. ID cards or credible identifying witness(es).
    b. ID cards or personal knowledge of identity.
    c. A credible identifying witness or personal knowledge of identity.

5. It is always forbidden for a Notary to …
   a. Take an acknowledgment over the phone.
   b. Notarize for a first cousin.
   c. Notarize for a blind person.

Fill in the Blank. Write in the word or phrase that best completes each sentence. Each correct answer is worth four points.

1. The Notary and the Notary's _____ are liable for the Notary's neglect or official misconduct.

2. A solemn, spoken pledge that is not an affirmation is called an _____.

3. An acceptable ID card should contain a signature, a description and a _____ of its bearer.

4. A certified copy certifies the _____ of the reproduction.

5. Wills written entirely in the testator's own handwriting are called _____.

Essay. Reply to each question or statement with a short paragraph. Each complete and correct response is worth eight points.

1. Discuss the distinctions between a Notary bond and Notary errors and omissions insurance.

2. Why is a Social Security Card all but worthless as an ID?

3. What is an apostille and when is it used?

4. Why should a Notary always complete the journal entry before filling out a notarial certificate?

5. Describe the differences between an acknowledgment certificate and a jurat certificate.

Test Answers
True/False. 1. F; 2. F; 3 T; 4. F; 5. T; 6. T; 7. F; 8. F; 9. F; 10. T; 11. F; 12. F; 13. F; 14. T; 15. F; 16. T; 17. T; 18. T; 19. F; 20. T

Multiple Choice. 1. c; 2. b; 3. c; 4. a; 5. a

Fill In The Blank. 1. Surety; 2. Oath; 3. Photograph; 4. Accuracy; 5. Holographic

Essay. Responses should include the basic information in the paragraphs below:

1. A Notary bond, obtained through a state-licensed surety company, provides protection for the public in case of the Notary's negligence or intentional misconduct. Up to the cash limit of the bond — $7,500 in Florida — the surety agrees to pay damages to anyone who suffers a loss because of the Notary's actions. The Notary, however, must then reimburse the surety. Notary errors and omissions insurance, also purchased from a state-licensed company, protects the Notary in case of an unintentional error, up to the policy limit. The Notary does not reimburse the insurance company. A bond is required by Florida law; errors and omissions insurance is not.

2. Florida law specifically lists what ID cards are acceptable and a Social Security Card is not among them. A Social Security Card is very easily counterfeited and has only one of the elements of a good ID, a signature. Reliable IDs should also bear a photograph and physical description.

3. An *apostille* is a certificate authenticating the signature and seal of a Notary. It is issued under provisions of an international treaty, signed by more than 80 nations, called the *Hague Convention Abolishing the Requirement of Legalization for Foreign Public Documents*. For notarized documents exchanged between the subscribing nations, this treaty streamlines the time-consuming authentication process known as "chain certification" by requiring only one authenticating certificate, the *apostille* (French for "notation"). *Apostilles* for Florida Notaries are issued by the Department of State.

4. Filling out a journal entry before completing a notarial certificate prevents a signer from leaving with the document

before an important record of the notarization is made in the journal.

5. An acknowledgment certificate certifies that the signer of the document personally appeared before the Notary on the date and in the county indicated. It also certifies that the signer's identity was satisfactorily proven to the Notary and that the signer acknowledged having signed freely. A jurat certifies that the person signing the document did so in the Notary's presence, that the person appeared before the Notary on the date and in the county indicated, that the person was positively identified by the Notary and that the Notary administered an oath or affirmation to the signer.

Tally Your Score

After checking your answers, add up your score. Then look at the grading scale below to determine how you stand:

- 90–100:   Excellent!
- 80–89:   Good, but some review needed.
- 70–79:   Fair. Reread the parts of the Primer covering the answers that you missed.
- Below 70: Below par. Study the laws thoroughly again. ■

Florida Laws Pertaining to Notaries Public

Reprinted on the following pages are pertinent parts of the Florida Statutes affecting Notaries and notarial acts.

These reprinted statutes are updated to include legislation effective July 1, 2008. For additional reference, history notes are included at the end of each section to show the source of the latest amendment to that section's text.

FLORIDA STATUTES

Title X. Public Officers, Employees, and Records
Chapter 117. Notaries Public

117.01   Appointment, application, suspension, revocation, application fee, bond, and oath.

117.03   Administration of oaths.

117.04   Acknowledgments.

117.045 Marriages.

117.05   Use of notary commission; unlawful use; notary fee; seal; duties; employer liability; name change; advertising; photocopies; penalties.

117.06   Validity of acts prior to April 1, 1903.

117.10   Law enforcement and correctional officers.

117.103 Certification of notary's authority by Secretary of State.

117.105 False or fraudulent acknowledgments; penalty.

117.107   Prohibited acts.
117.108   Validity of acts, seals, and certificates prior to January 1, 1995.

117.01. Appointment, application, suspension, revocation, application fee, bond, and oath.—

(1) The Governor may appoint as many notaries public as he or she deems necessary, each of whom shall be at least 18 years of age and a legal resident of the state. A permanent resident alien may apply and be appointed and shall file with his or her application a recorded Declaration of Domicile. The residence required for appointment must be maintained throughout the term of appointment. Notaries public shall be appointed for 4 years and shall use and exercise the office of notary public within the boundaries of this state. An applicant must be able to read, write, and understand the English language.

(2) The application for appointment shall be signed and sworn to by the applicant and shall be accompanied by a fee of $25, together with the $10 commission fee required by s. 113.01, and a surcharge of $4, which $4 is appropriated to the Executive Office of the Governor to be used to educate and assist notaries public. The Executive Office of the Governor may contract with private vendors to provide the services set forth in this section. However, no commission fee shall be required for the issuance of a commission as a notary public to a veteran who served during a period of wartime service, as defined in s. 1.01(14), and who has been rated by the United States Government or the United States Department of Veterans Affairs or its predecessor to have a disability rating of 50 percent or more; such a disability is subject to verification by the Secretary of State, who has authority to adopt reasonable procedures to implement this act. The oath of office and notary bond required by this section shall also accompany the application and shall be in a form prescribed by the Department of State which shall require, but not be limited to, the following information: full name, residence address and telephone number, business address and telephone number, date of birth, race, sex, social security number, citizenship status, driver's license number or the number of other official state-issued identification, affidavit of good character from someone unrelated to the applicant who has known the applicant for 1 year or more, a list of all professional licenses and commissions issued by the state during the previous 10 years and a statement as to whether or not the applicant has had such license or commission revoked or suspended, and a statement as to whether or not the applicant has been convicted of a felony, and, if there has been a conviction, a statement of the nature of the felony and restoration of civil rights. The applicant may not use a fictitious or assumed name other than a nickname on an application for commission. The application shall be maintained by the Department of State for the full term of a notary commission. A notary public shall notify, in writing, the Department of State of any change in his or her business address, home telephone number, business telephone number, home address, or criminal record within 60 days after such change. The Governor may require any other information he or she deems necessary for determining whether an

applicant is eligible for a notary public commission. Each applicant must swear or affirm on the application that the information on the application is true and correct.

(3) As part of the oath, the applicant must swear that he or she has read this chapter and knows the duties, responsibilities, limitations, and powers of a notary public.

(4) The Governor may suspend a notary public for any of the grounds provided in s. 7, Art. IV of the State Constitution. Grounds constituting malfeasance, misfeasance, or neglect of duty include, but are not limited to, the following:

(a) A material false statement on the application.

(b) A complaint found to have merit by the Governor.

(c) Failure to cooperate or respond to an investigation by the Governor's office or the Department of State regarding a complaint.

(d) Official misconduct as defined in s. 838.022.

(e) False or misleading advertising relating to notary public services.

(f) Unauthorized practice of law.

(g) Failure to report a change in business or home address or telephone number, or failure to submit documentation to request an amended commission after a lawful name change, within the specified period of time.

(h) Commission of fraud, misrepresentation, or any intentional violation of this chapter.

(i) Charging fees in excess of fees authorized by this chapter.

(j) Failure to maintain the bond required by this section.

(5)(a) If a notary public receives notice from the Department of State that his or her office has been declared vacant, the notary shall forthwith mail or deliver to the Secretary of State his or her notary commission.

(b) A notary public who wishes to resign his or her commission, or a notary public who does not maintain legal residence in this state during the entire term of appointment, or a notary public whose resignation is required by the Governor, shall send a signed letter of resignation to the Governor and shall return his or her certificate of notary public commission. The resigning notary public shall destroy his or her official notary public seal of office, unless the Governor requests its return.

(6) No person may be automatically reappointed as a notary public. The application process must be completed regardless of whether an applicant is requesting his or her first notary commission, a renewal of a commission, or any subsequent commission.

(7)(a) A notary public shall, prior to executing the duties of the office and throughout the term of office, give bond, payable to any individual harmed as a result of a breach of duty by the notary public acting in his or her official capacity, in the amount of $7,500, conditioned for the due discharge of the office and shall take an oath that he or she will honestly, diligently, and faithfully discharge the duties of the notary public. The bond shall be approved and filed with the Department of State and executed by a surety company for hire duly authorized to transact business in this state.

(b) Any notary public whose term of appointment extends beyond January 1, 1999, is required to increase the amount of his or her bond to

$7,500 only upon reappointment on or after January 1, 1999.

(c) Beginning July 1, 1996, surety companies for hire which process notary public applications, oaths, affidavits of character, and bonds for submission to the Department of State must properly submit these documents in a software and hard copy format approved by the Department of State.

(8) Upon payment to any individual harmed as a result of a breach of duty by the notary public, the entity who has issued the bond for the notary public shall notify the Governor of the payment and the circumstances which led to the claim.

History.--s. 1, Sept. 13, 1822; RS 218; s. 1, ch. 4544, 1897; GS 302; RGS 413; CGL 479; s. 1, ch. 21765, 1943; s. 1, ch. 63-138; s. 1, ch. 65-256; ss. 1, 2, ch. 67-54; ss. 10, 12, 35, ch. 69-106; s. 70, ch. 71-136; s. 1, ch. 75-161; s. 6, ch. 77-121; ss. 5, 6, ch. 81-260; s. 33, ch. 83-217; s. 3, ch. 88-557; s. 1, ch. 91-291; s. 1, ch. 92-209; s. 746, ch. 95-147; s. 18, ch. 95-280; s. 27, ch. 95-312; s. 2, ch. 96-407; s. 1, ch. 98-246; s. 9, ch. 2003-158.

117.03 Administration of oaths.— A notary public may administer an oath and make a certificate thereof when it is necessary for the execution of any writing or document to be published under the seal of a notary public. The notary public may not take an acknowledgment of execution in lieu of an oath if an oath is required.

History.—s. 1, Sept. 13, 1822; RS 219; GS 304; RGS 415; CGL 481; s. 20, ch. 73-334; s. 1, ch. 80-173; s. 2, ch. 91-291; s. 2, ch. 92-209; s. 2, ch. 93-62; s. 2, ch. 98-246.

117.04 Acknowledgments.— A notary public is authorized to take the acknowledgments of deeds and other instruments of writing for record, as fully as other officers of this state.

History.—s. 2, ch. 1127, 1860; RS 220; GS 305; RGS 416; CGL 482; s. 20, ch. 73-334; s. 8, ch. 81-260; s. 3, ch. 91-291; s. 3, ch. 93-62; s. 3, ch. 98-246.

117.045 Marriages.— A notary public is authorized to solemnize the rites of matrimony. For solemnizing the rites of matrimony, the fee of a notary public may not exceed those provided by law to the clerks of the circuit court for like services.

History.—s. 4, ch. 98-246.

117.05 Use of notary commission; unlawful use; notary fee; seal; duties; employer liability; name change; advertising; photocopies; penalties.—

(1) No person shall obtain or use a notary public commission in other than his or her legal name, and it is unlawful for a notary public to notarize his or her own signature. Any person applying for a notary public commission must submit proof of identity to the Department of State if so requested. Any person who violates the provisions of this subsection is guilty of a felony of the third degree, punishable as provided in s. 775.082, s. 775.083, or s. 775.084.

(2)(a) The fee of a notary public may not exceed $10 for any one notarial act, except as provided in s. 117.045.

(b) A notary public may not charge a fee for witnessing an absentee ballot in an election, and must witness such a ballot upon the request of an elector, provided the notarial act is in accordance with the provisions of this chapter.

(3)(a) A notary public seal shall be affixed to all notarized paper documents and shall be of the rubber stamp type and shall include the words "Notary Public-State of Florida." The seal shall also include the name of the notary public, the date of expiration of the commission of the notary public, and the commission number. The rubber stamp seal must be affixed to the notarized paper document in photographically reproducible black ink. Every notary public shall print, type, or stamp below his or her signature on a paper document his or her name exactly as commissioned. An impression-type seal may be used in addition to the rubber stamp seal, but the rubber stamp seal shall be the official seal for use on a paper document, and the impression-type seal may not be substituted therefor.

(b) Any notary public whose term of appointment extends beyond January 1, 1992, is required to use a rubber stamp type notary public seal on paper documents only upon reappointment on or after January 1, 1992.

(c) The notary public official seal and the certificate of notary public commission are the exclusive property of the notary public and must be kept under the direct and exclusive control of the notary public. The seal and certificate of commission must not be surrendered to an employer upon termination of employment, regardless of whether the employer paid for the seal or for the commission.

(d) A notary public whose official seal is lost, stolen, or believed to be in the possession of another person shall immediately notify the Department of State or the Governor in writing.

(e) Any person who unlawfully possesses a notary public official seal or any papers or copies relating to notarial acts is guilty of a misdemeanor of the second degree, punishable as provided in s. 775.082 or s. 775.083.

(4) When notarizing a signature, a notary public shall complete a jurat or notarial certificate in substantially the same form as those found in subsection (13). The jurat or certificate of acknowledgment shall contain the following elements:

(a) The venue stating the location of the notarization in the format, "State of Florida, County of _____."

(b) The type of notarial act performed, an oath or an acknowledgment, evidenced by the words "sworn" or "acknowledged."

(c) That the signer personally appeared before the notary public at the time of the notarization.

(d) The exact date of the notarial act.

(e) The name of the person whose signature is being notarized. It is presumed, absent such specific notation by the notary public, that notarization is to all signatures.

(f) The specific type of identification the notary public is relying upon in identifying the signer, either based on personal knowledge or satisfactory evidence specified in subsection (5).

(g) The notary's official signature.

(h) The notary's name, typed, printed, or stamped below the signature.

(i) The notary's official seal affixed below or to either side of the notary's signature.

(5) A notary public may not notarize a signature on a document unless he or she personally knows, or has satisfactory evidence, that the person whose signature is to be notarized is the individual who is described in and who is executing the instrument. A notary public shall certify in the certificate of acknowledgment or jurat the type of identification, either based on personal knowledge or other form of identification, upon which the notary public is relying.

(a) For purposes of this subsection, "personally knows" means having an acquaintance, derived from association with the individual, which establishes the individual's identity with at least a reasonable certainty.

(b) For the purposes of this subsection, "satisfactory evidence" means the absence of any information, evidence, or other circumstances which would lead a reasonable person to believe that the person whose signature is to be notarized is not the person he or she claims to be and any one of the following:

1. The sworn written statement of one credible witness personally known to the notary public or the sworn written statement of two credible witnesses whose identities are proven to the notary public upon the presentation of satisfactory evidence that each of the following is true:

a. That the person whose signature is to be notarized is the person named in the document;

b. That the person whose signature is to be notarized is personally known to the witnesses;

c. That it is the reasonable belief of the witnesses that the circumstances of the person whose signature is to be notarized are such that it would be very difficult or impossible for that person to obtain another acceptable form of identification;

d. That it is the reasonable belief of the witnesses that the person whose signature is to be notarized does not possess any of the identification documents specified in subparagraph 2.; and

e. That the witnesses do not have a financial interest in nor are parties to the underlying transaction; or

2. Reasonable reliance on the presentation to the notary public of any one of the following forms of identification, if the document is current or has been issued within the past 5 years and bears a serial or other identifying number:

a. A Florida identification card or driver's license issued by the public agency authorized to issue driver's licenses;

b. A passport issued by the Department of State of the United States;

c. A passport issued by a foreign government if the document is stamped by the United States Bureau of Citizenship and Immigration Services;

d. A driver's license or an identification card issued by a public agency authorized to issue driver's licenses in a state other than Florida, a territory of the United States, or Canada or Mexico;

e. An identification card issued by any branch of the armed forces of the United States;

f. An inmate identification card issued on or after January 1, 1991, by the Florida Department of Corrections for an inmate who is in the custody of the department;

g. An inmate identification card issued by the United States Department of Justice, Bureau of Prisons, for an inmate who is in the custody of the department;

h. A sworn, written statement from a sworn law enforcement officer that the forms of identification for an inmate in an institution of confinement were confiscated upon confinement and that the person named in the document is the person whose signature is to be notarized; or

i. An identification card issued by the United States Bureau of Citizenship and Immigration Services.

(6) The employer of a notary public shall be liable to the persons involved for all damages proximately caused by the notary's official misconduct, if the notary public was acting within the scope of his or her employment at the time the notary engaged in the official misconduct.

(7) Any person who acts as or otherwise willfully impersonates a notary public while not lawfully appointed and commissioned to perform notarial acts is guilty of a misdemeanor of the second degree, punishable as provided in s. 775.082 or s. 775.083.

(8) Any notary public who knowingly acts as a notary public after his or her commission has expired is guilty of a misdemeanor of the second degree, punishable as provided in s. 775.082 or s. 775.083.

(9) Any notary public who lawfully changes his or her name shall, within 60 days after such change, request an amended commission from the Secretary of State and shall send $25, his or her current commission, and a notice of change form, obtained from the Secretary of State, which shall include the new name and contain a specimen of his or her official signature. The Secretary of State shall issue an amended commission to the notary public in the new name. A rider to the notary public's bond must accompany the notice of change form. After submitting the required notice of change form and rider to the Secretary of State, the notary public may continue to perform notarial acts in his or her former name for 60 days or until receipt of the amended commission, whichever date is earlier.

(10) A notary public who is not an attorney who advertises the services of a notary public in a language other than English, whether by radio, television, signs, pamphlets, newspapers, or other written communication, with the exception of a single desk plaque, shall post or otherwise include with the advertisement a notice in English and in the language used for the advertisement. The notice shall be of a conspicuous size, if in writing, and shall state: "I AM NOT AN ATTORNEY LICENSED TO PRACTICE LAW IN THE STATE OF FLORIDA, AND I MAY NOT GIVE LEGAL ADVICE OR ACCEPT FEES FOR LEGAL ADVICE." If the advertisement is by radio or television, the statement may be modified but must include substantially the same message.

(11) Literal translation of the phrase "Notary Public" into a language other than English is prohibited in an advertisement for notarial services.

(12)(a) A notary public may supervise the making of a photocopy of an original document and attest to the trueness of the copy, provided the document is neither a vital record in this state, another state, a territory of the United States, or another country, nor a public record, if a copy can be made by the custodian of the public record.

(b) A notary public must use a certificate in substantially the following form in notarizing an attested copy:

STATE OF FLORIDA
COUNTY OF _____

On this _____ day of _____, (year), I attest that the preceding or attached document is a true, exact, complete, and unaltered photocopy made by me of (description of document) presented to me by the document's custodian, _____, and, to the best of my knowledge, that the photocopied document is neither a vital record nor a public record, certified copies of which are available from an official source other than a notary public.

_____ (Official Notary Signature and Notary Seal)
_____ (Name of Notary Typed, Printed or Stamped)

(13) The following notarial certificates are sufficient for the purposes indicated, if completed with the information required by this chapter. The specification of forms under this subsection does not preclude the use of other forms.

(a) For an oath or affirmation:

STATE OF FLORIDA
COUNTY OF _____

Sworn to (or affirmed) and subscribed before me this _____ day of _____, (year), by (name of person making statement).

_____ (Signature of Notary Public - State of Florida)
_____ (Print, Type, or Stamp Commissioned Name of Notary Public)
Personally Known _____ OR Produced Identification _____
Type of Identification Produced _____

(b) For an acknowledgment in an individual capacity:

STATE OF FLORIDA
COUNTY OF _____

The foregoing instrument was acknowledged before me this _____ day of _____, (year), by (name of person acknowledging).
_____ (Signature of Notary Public - State of Florida)
_____ (Print, Type, or Stamp Commissioned Name of Notary Public)
Personally Known _____ OR Produced Identification _____
Type of Identification Produced _____

(c) For an acknowledgment in a representative capacity:

STATE OF FLORIDA
COUNTY OF _____

The foregoing instrument was acknowledged before me this _____ day of _____, (year), by (name of person) as (type of authority, e.g. officer, trustee, attorney-in-fact) for (name of party on behalf of whom instrument was executed).

_____ (Signature of Notary Public - State of Florida)
_____ (Print, Type, or Stamp Commissioned Name of Notary Public)
Personally Known _____ OR Produced Identification _____
Type of Identification Produced _____

(14) A notary public must make reasonable accommodations to provide notarial services to persons with disabilities.

(a) A notary public may notarize the signature of a person who is blind after the notary public has read the entire instrument to that person.

(b) A notary public may notarize the signature of a person who signs with a mark if:

1. The document signing is witnessed by two disinterested persons;

2. The notary prints the person's first name at the beginning of the designated signature line and the person's last name at the end of the designated signature line; and

3. The notary prints the words "his (or her) mark" below the person's signature mark.

(c) The following notarial certificates are sufficient for the purpose of notarizing for a person who signs with a mark:

1. For an oath or affirmation:

_____ (First Name) _____ (Last Name)
_____ His (or Her) Mark

STATE OF FLORIDA
COUNTY OF _____

Sworn to and subscribed before me this _____ day of _____, (year), by (name of person making statement), who signed with a mark in the presence of these witnesses:
_____ (Signature of Notary Public - State of Florida)
_____ (Print, Type, or Stamp Commissioned Name of Notary Public)
Personally Known _____ OR Produced Identification _____
Type of Identification Produced _____

2. For an acknowledgment in an individual capacity:

_____ (First Name) _____ (Last Name)
_____ His (or Her) Mark

STATE OF FLORIDA
COUNTY OF _____

The foregoing instrument was acknowledged before me this _____ day of

_____, (year), by (name of person acknowledging), who signed with a mark in the presence of these witnesses:

_____ (Signature of Notary Public - State of Florida)
_____ (Print, Type, or Stamp Commissioned Name of Notary Public)
Personally Known _____ OR Produced Identification _____
Type of Identification Produced _____

(d) A notary public may sign the name of a person whose signature is to be notarized when that person is physically unable to sign or make a signature mark on a document if:

1. The person with a disability directs the notary to sign in his or her presence;

2. The document signing is witnessed by two disinterested persons;

3. The notary writes below the signature the following statement: "Signature affixed by notary, pursuant to s. 117.05(14), Florida Statutes," and states the circumstances of the signing in the notarial certificate.

(e) The following notarial certificates are sufficient for the purpose of notarizing for a person with a disability who directs the notary to sign his or her name:

1. For an oath or affirmation:

STATE OF FLORIDA
COUNTY OF _____

Sworn to (or affirmed) before me this _____ day of _____, (year), by (name of person making statement), and subscribed by (name of notary) at the direction of and in the presence of (name of person making statement), and in the presence of these witnesses:
_____ (Signature of Notary Public - State of Florida)
_____ (Print, Type, or Stamp Commissioned Name of Notary Public)
Personally Known _____ OR Produced Identification _____
Type of Identification Produced _____

2. For an acknowledgment in an individual capacity:

STATE OF FLORIDA
COUNTY OF _____

The foregoing instrument was acknowledged before me this _____ day of _____, (year), by (name of person acknowledging) and subscribed by (name of notary) at the direction of and in the presence of (name of person acknowledging), and in the presence of these witnesses:

_____ (Signature of Notary Public - State of Florida)
_____ (Print, Type, or Stamp Commissioned Name of Notary Public)
Personally Known _____ OR Produced Identification _____
Type of Identification Produced _____

History.--ch. 3874, 1889; RS 221; GS 306; RGS 417; CGL 483; s. 8, ch.

81-260; s. 4, ch. 91-291; s. 3, ch. 92-209; s. 4, ch. 93-62; s. 747, ch. 95-147; s. 1, ch. 97-241; s. 33, ch. 98-129; s. 5, ch. 98-246; s. 46, ch. 99-2; s. 7, ch. 2004-5.

117.06 Validity of acts prior to April 1, 1903.— Any and all notarial acts that were done by any notary public in the state prior to April 1, 1903, which would have been valid had not the term of office of the notary public expired, are declared to be valid.

History.—s. 1, ch. 5217, 1903; GS 307; RGS 418; CGL 484.

117.10 Law enforcement and correctional officers.— Law enforcement officers, correctional officers, and correctional probation officers, as defined in s. 943.10, and traffic accident investigation officers and traffic infraction enforcement officers, as described in s. 316.640, are authorized to administer oaths when engaged in the performance of official duties. Sections 117.01, 117.04, 117.045, 117.05, and 117.103 do not apply to the provisions of this section. An officer may not notarize his or her own signature.

History.—s. 4, ch. 84-97; s. 43, ch. 89-526; s. 2, ch. 91-174; s. 9, ch. 91-291; s. 748, ch. 95-147; s. 4, ch. 95-283; s. 6, ch. 98-246.

117.021 Electronic notarization.--

(1) Any document requiring notarization may be notarized electronically. The provisions of ss. 117.01, 117.03, 117.04, 117.05(1)-(11), (13), and (14), 117.105, and 117.107 apply to all notarizations under this section.

(2) In performing an electronic notarial act, a notary public shall use an electronic signature that is:

(a) Unique to the notary public;

(b) Capable of independent verification;

(c) Retained under the notary public's sole control; and

(d) Attached to or logically associated with the electronic document in a manner that any subsequent alteration to the electronic document displays evidence of the alteration.

(3) When a signature is required to be accompanied by a notary public seal, the requirement is satisfied when the electronic signature of the notary public contains all of the following seal information:

(a) The full name of the notary public exactly as provided on the notary public's application for commission;

(b) The words "Notary Public State of Florida";

(c) The date of expiration of the commission of the notary public; and

(d) The notary public's commission number.

(4) Failure of a notary public to comply with any of the requirements of this section may constitute grounds for suspension of the notary public's commission by the Executive Office of the Governor.

(5) The Department of State may adopt rules to ensure the security, reliability, and uniformity of signatures and seals authorized in this section.

117.103 Certification of notary's authority by Secretary of State.— A notary public is not required to record his or her notary public commission in an office of a clerk of the circuit court. If certification of the notary public's commission is required, it must be obtained from the Secretary of State. Upon the receipt of a written request and a fee of $10 payable to the Secretary of State, the Secretary of State shall issue a certificate of notarial authority, in a form prescribed by the Secretary of State, which shall include a statement explaining the legal qualifications and authority of a notary public in this state.

History.—s. 5, ch. 91-291; s. 7, ch. 98-246; s. 72, ch. 99-251.

117.105 False or fraudulent acknowledgments; penalty.— A notary public who falsely or fraudulently takes an acknowledgment of an instrument as a notary public or who falsely or fraudulently makes a certificate as a notary public or who falsely takes or receives an acknowledgment of the signature on a written instrument is guilty of a felony of the third degree, punishable as provided in s. 775.082, s. 775.083, or s. 775.084.

History.—s. 6, ch. 91-291.

117.107 Prohibited acts.—

(1) A notary public may not use a name or initial in signing certificates other than that by which the notary public is commissioned.

(2) A notary public may not sign notarial certificates using a facsimile signature stamp unless the notary public has a physical disability that limits or prohibits his or her ability to make a written signature and unless the notary public has first submitted written notice to the Department of State with an exemplar of the facsimile signature stamp.

(3) A notary public may not affix his or her signature to a blank form of affidavit or certificate of acknowledgment and deliver that form to another person with the intent that it be used as an affidavit or acknowledgment.

(4) A notary public may not take the acknowledgment of or administer an oath to a person whom the notary public actually knows to have been adjudicated mentally incapacitated by a court of competent jurisdiction, where the acknowledgment or oath necessitates the exercise of a right that has been removed pursuant to s. 744.3215(2) or (3), and where the person has not been restored to capacity as a matter of record.

(5) A notary public may not notarize a signature on a document if it appears that the person is mentally incapable of understanding the nature and effect of the document at the time of notarization.

(6) A notary public may not take the acknowledgment of a person who does not speak or understand the English language, unless the nature and effect of the instrument to be notarized is translated into a language which the person does understand.

(7) A notary public may not change anything in a written instrument after it has been signed by anyone.

(8) A notary public may not amend a notarial certificate after the notarization is complete.

(9) A notary public may not notarize a signature on a document if the person whose signature is being notarized is not in the presence of the notary public at the time the signature is notarized. Any notary public who violates this subsection is guilty of a civil infraction, punishable by penalty not exceeding $5,000, and such violation constitutes malfeasance and misfeasance in the conduct of official duties. It is no defense to the civil infraction specified in this subsection that the notary public acted without

intent to defraud. A notary public who violates this subsection with the intent to defraud is guilty of violating s. 117.105.

(10) A notary public may not notarize a signature on a document if the document is incomplete or blank. However, an endorsement or assignment in blank of a negotiable or nonnegotiable note and the assignment in blank of any instrument given as security for such note is not deemed incomplete.

(11) A notary public may not notarize a signature on a document if the person whose signature is to be notarized is the spouse, son, daughter, mother, or father of the notary public.

(12) A notary public may not notarize a signature on a document if the notary public has a financial interest in or is a party to the underlying transaction; however, a notary public who is an employee may notarize a signature for his or her employer, and this employment does not constitute a financial interest in the transaction nor make the notary a party to the transaction under this subsection as long as he or she does not receive a benefit other than his or her salary and the fee for services as a notary public authorized by law. For purposes of this subsection, a notary public who is an attorney does not have a financial interest in and is not a party to the underlying transaction evidenced by a notarized document if he or she notarizes a signature on that document for a client for whom he or she serves as an attorney of record and he or she has no interest in the document other than the fee paid to him or her for legal services and the fee authorized by law for services as a notary public.

History.—s. 7, ch. 91-291; s. 4, ch. 92-209; s. 749, ch. 95-147; s. 19, ch. 95-280; s. 8, ch. 98-246.

117.108 Validity of acts, seals, and certificates prior to January 1, 1995.— A notarial act performed, a notarial certificate signed, or a notarial seal used by any notary public before January 1, 1995, which would have been valid under the laws in effect in this state on January 1, 1991, is valid.

History.—s. 5, ch. 93-62.

IMPORTANT NOTICE — Electronic Notarization Repealed. The short-lived former provision of the Florida Statutes (§117.20) authorizing Notaries with amended commissions to perform "electronic notarizations" was repealed with enactment of Senate Bill 1566 in 1999 (Chapter 99-251). This repeal deletes statute language originally enacted in 1997 (Chapter 97-241) and revised in 1998 (Chapter 98-246).

Title V. Judicial Branch
Chapter 28. Clerks of the Circuit Courts

28.24 Service charges by clerk of the circuit court.— The clerk of the circuit court may charge for services rendered by the clerk's office in recording documents and instruments and in performing the duties enumerated in amounts not to exceed those specified in this section. Notwithstanding any other provision of this section, the clerk of the circuit court shall provide without charge to the state attorney, public defender, and guardian ad litem, and to the authorized staff acting on behalf of each, access to and a copy of any public record, if the requesting party is entitled by law to view the exempt or confidential record, as maintained by and in the custody of the clerk of the circuit court as provided in general law and the Florida Rules of Judicial Administration. The clerk of the circuit court may provide the requested public record in an electronic format in lieu of a paper format when capable of being accessed by the requesting entity.

Charges

***

(3) For certifying copies of any instrument in the public records....... 1

(4) For verifying any instrument presented for certification prepared by someone other than clerk, per page....... 2

***

(15) For preparing affidavit of domicile....... 5

***

(17) For authenticated certificates, including signing and sealing....... 4

***

(23) Upon receipt of an application for a marriage license, for preparing and administering of oath; issuing, sealing, and recording of the marriage license; and providing a certified copy....... 30

(24) For solemnizing matrimony....... 30

***

History.--s. 1, ch. 3106, 1879; RS 1394; GS 1839; RGS 3084; ss. 1, 2, ch. 11893, 1927; CGL 4867; s. 2, ch. 29749, 1955; s. 1, ch. 63-45; s. 5, ch. 70-134; s. 1, ch. 77-284; s. 1, ch. 78-367; s. 1, ch. 79-266; s. 12, ch. 79-400; s. 1, ch. 82-205; s. 35, ch. 85-180; s. 2, ch. 85-249; s. 22, ch. 87-95; s. 2, ch. 87-145; s. 1, ch. 88-176; s. 1, ch. 92-200; ss. 5, 13, ch. 94-348; s. 5, ch. 95-214; s. 2, ch. 2000-144; s. 90, ch. 2003-261; s. 28, ch. 2003-402; s. 16, ch. 2004-265; ch. 2005-236.

Title X. Public Officers, Employees, and Records
Chapter 118. International Notaries

118.10 Civil-law notary.—

(1) As used in this section, the term:

(a) "Authentic act" means an instrument executed by a civil-law notary referencing this section, which instrument includes the particulars and capacities to act of any transacting parties, a confirmation of the full text of any necessary instrument, the signatures or their legal equivalent of any transacting parties, the signature and seal of a civil-law notary, and such other information prescribed by the Secretary of State.

(b) "Civil-law notary" means a person who is a member in good standing of The Florida Bar, who has practiced law for at least 5 years, and who is appointed by the Secretary of State as a civil-law notary.

(c) "Protocol" means a registry maintained by a civil-law notary in which the acts of the civil-law notary are archived.

(2) The Secretary of State shall have the power to appoint civil-law notaries and administer this section.

(3) A civil-law notary is authorized to issue authentic acts and thereby may authenticate or certify any document, transaction, event, condition, or occurrence. The contents of an authentic act and matters incorporated therein shall be presumed correct. A civil-law notary may also administer an oath and make a certificate thereof when it is necessary for execution of any writing or document to be attested, protested, or published under the seal of a notary public. A civil-law notary may also take acknowledgements of deeds and other instruments of writing for record, and solemnize the rites of matrimony, as fully as other officers of this state. A civil-law notary is not authorized to issue authentic acts for use in a jurisdiction if the United States Department of State has determined that the jurisdiction does not have diplomatic relations with the United States or is a terrorist country, or if trade with the jurisdiction is prohibited under the Trading With the Enemy Act of 1917, as amended, 50 U.S.C. ss. 1, et seq.

(4) The authentic acts, oaths and acknowledgements, and solemnizations of a civil-law notary shall be recorded in the civil-law notary's protocol in a manner prescribed by the Secretary of State.

(5) The Secretary of State may adopt rules prescribing:

(a) The form and content of authentic acts, oaths, acknowledgments, solemnizations, and signatures and seals or their legal equivalents;

(b) Procedures for the permanent archiving of authentic acts, maintaining records of acknowledgments, oaths and solemnizations, and procedures for the administration of oaths and taking of acknowledgments;

(c) The charging of reasonable fees to be retained by the Secretary of State for the purpose of administering this chapter;

(d) Educational requirements and procedures for testing applicants' knowledge of all materials relevant to the appointment, authority, duties or legal or ethical responsibilities of a civil-law notary;

(e) Procedures for the disciplining of civil-law notaries, including, but not limited to, the suspension and revocation of appointments for failure to comply with the requirements of Chapter 118 or the rules of the Department of State, or for misrepresentation or fraud regarding the civil-law notary's authority, the effect of the civil-law notary's authentic acts, or the identities or acts of the parties to a transaction;

(f) Bonding or errors and omissions insurance requirements, or both, for civil-law notaries; and

(g) Other matters necessary for administering this section.

(6) The Secretary of State shall not regulate, discipline, or attempt to discipline any civil-law notary for, or with regard to, any action or conduct that would constitute the practice of law in this state, except by agreement with The Florida Bar. The Secretary of State shall not establish as a prerequisite to the appointment of a civil-law notary any test containing any question that inquires of the applicant's knowledge regarding the practice of law in the United States, unless such test is offered in conjunction with an educational program approved by The Florida Bar for continuing legal education credit.

(7) The powers of civil-law notaries include, but are not limited to, all of the powers of a notary public under any law of this state.

(8) This section shall not be construed as abrogating the provisions of any other act relating to notaries public, attorneys, or the practice of law in this state.

History.—s. 7, ch. 97-241; s. 1, ch. 97-278; ss. 10, 20, ch. 98-246; s.74, ch. 99-251.

118.12 Certificate of civil-law notary's authority; apostilles.— If certification of a civil-law notary's authority is necessary for a particular document or transaction, it must be obtained from the Secretary of State. Upon the receipt of a written request from a civil-law notary and the fee prescribed by the Secretary of State, the Secretary of State shall issue a certification of the civil-law notary's authority, in a form prescribed by the Secretary of State, which shall include a statement explaining the legal qualifications and authority of a civil-law notary in this state. The fee prescribed for the issuance of the certification under this section or an apostille under s. 15.16 may not exceed $10 per document. The Department of State may adopt rules to implement this section.

History.— s. 75, ch. 99-251.

Title XXXIX. Commercial Relations
Chapter 668. Electronic Commerce
Part I. Electronic Signatures

6681 Short title.— This act may be cited as the "Electronic Signature Act of 1996."

History.—s. 1, ch. 96-224.

6682 Legislative intent.— It is the intent of the Legislature that this act:

(1) Facilitate economic development and efficient delivery of government services by means of reliable electronic messages.

(2) Enhance public confidence in the use of electronic signatures.

(3) Minimize the incidence of forged electronic signatures and fraud in electronic commerce.

(4) Foster the development of electronic commerce through the use of electronic signatures to lend authenticity and integrity to writings in any electronic medium.

(5) Assure that proper management oversight and accountability are maintained for agency-conducted electronic commerce.

History.—s. 2, ch. 96-224.

6683 Definitions.— As used in this act:

(1) "Certificate" means a computer-based record which:

(a) Identifies the certification authority.

(b) Identifies the subscriber.

(c) Contains the subscriber's public key.

(d) Is digitally signed by the certification authority.

(2) "Certification authority" means a person who issues a certificate.

(3) "Digital signature" means a type of electronic signature that transforms a message using an asymmetric cryptosystem such that a person having the

initial message and the signer's public key can accurately determine:

(a) Whether the transformation was created using the private key that corresponds to the signer's public key.

(b) Whether the initial message has been altered since the transformation was made.

A "key pair" is a private key and its corresponding public key in an asymmetric cryptosystem, under which the public key verifies a digital signature the private key creates. An "asymmetric cryptosystem" is an algorithm or series of algorithms which provide a secure key pair.

(4) "Electronic signature" means any letters, characters, or symbols, manifested by electronic or similar means, executed or adopted by a party with an intent to authenticate a writing. A writing is electronically signed if an electronic signature is logically associated with such writing.

History.—s. 4, ch. 96-224.

6684 Force and effect of electronic signature.— Unless otherwise provided by law, an electronic signature may be used to sign a writing and shall have the same force and effect as a written signature.

History.—s. 5, ch. 96-224.

6686 Control procedures.—The head of each agency shall be responsible for adopting and implementing control processes and procedures to ensure adequate integrity, security, confidentiality, and auditability of business transactions conducted using electronic commerce.

History.—s. 7, ch. 96-224.

Title XXXIX. Commercial Relations
Chapter 668. Electronic Commerce
Part II. Uniform Electronic Transactions Act

****

668.50(ll) Notarization and Acknowledgment.—

(a) If a law requires a signature or record to be notarized, acknowledged, verified, or made under oath, the requirement is satisfied if the electronic signature of the person authorized by applicable law to perform these acts, together with all other information required to be included by other applicable law, is attached to or logically associated with the signature or record. Neither a rubber stamp nor an impression type seal is required for an electronic notarization.

(b) A first-time applicant for a notary commission must submit proof that the applicant has, within 1 year prior to the application, completed at least 3 hours of interactive or classroom instruction, including electronic notarization, and covering the duties of the notary public. Courses satisfying this section may be offered by any public or private sector person or entity registered with the Executive Office of the Governor and must include a core curriculum approved by that office.

****

Title XXIII. Motor Vehicles
Chapter 319. Title Certificates

319.23 Application for, and issuance of, certificate of title.—
***

(3) If a certificate of title has not previously been issued for a motor vehicle or mobile home in this state, the application, unless otherwise provided for in this chapter, shall be accompanied by a proper bill of sale or sworn statement of ownership, or a duly certified copy thereof, or by a certificate of title, bill of sale, or other evidence of ownership required by the law of the state or county from which the motor vehicle or mobile home was brought into this state. The application shall also be accompanied by:

(a)1. A sworn affidavit from the seller and purchaser verifying that the vehicle identification number shown on the affidavit is identical to the vehicle identification number shown on the motor vehicle; or

2. An appropriate departmental form evidencing that a physical examination has been made of the motor vehicle by the owner and by a duly constituted law enforcement officer in any state, a licensed motor vehicle dealer, a license inspector as provided by s. 320.58, or a notary public commissioned by this state and that the vehicle identification number shown on such form is identical to the vehicle identification number shown on the motor vehicle; and

(b) If the vehicle is a used car original, a sworn affidavit from the owner verifying that the odometer reading shown on the affidavit is identical to the odometer reading shown on the motor vehicle in accordance with the requirements of 49 C.F.R. s. 580.5 at the time that application for title is made. For the purposes of this section, the term "used car original" means a used vehicle coming into and being titled in this state for the first time.

(c) If the vehicle is an ancient, antique, or collectible vehicle as defined in s. 320.086, the application shall be accompanied either by a certificate of title; a notarized bill of sale and a registration; or a notarized bill of sale, an affidavit by the owner defending the title from all claims. The bill of sale must contain a complete vehicle description to include the vehicle identification or engine number, year make, color, selling price, and signatures of the seller and purchaser.
***

History.—s. 4, ch. 23658, 1947; s. 3, ch. 25150, 1949; s. 1, ch. 28184, 1953; s. 2, ch. 61-296; s. 6, ch. 65-190; ss. 24, 35, ch. 69-106; s. 1, ch. 72-15; s. 2, ch. 75-66; s. 1, ch. 77-102; s. 4, ch. 78-221; s. 1, ch. 78-225; s. 2, ch. 78-412; s. 1, ch. 79-32; s. 1, ch. 79-399; s. 1, ch. 80-388; s. 7, ch. 82-134; s. 2, ch. 83-91; s. 42, ch. 85-180; s. 7, ch. 88-306; s. 1, ch. 89-53; ss. 12, 16, ch. 89-333; s. 339, ch. 95-148; ss. 13, 21, ch. 96-413.

Title XXXII. Regulation of Professions and Occupations
Chapter 454. Attorneys at Law

454.23 Penalties.— Any person not licensed or otherwise authorized to practice law in this state who practices law in this state or holds himself or herself out to the public as qualified to practice law in this state, or who willfully pretends to be, or willfully takes or uses any name, title, addition, or description implying that he or she is qualified, or recognized by law as qualified, to practice law in this state, commits a felony of the third degree, punishable as provided in s. 775.082, s. 775.083, or s. 775.084.

History.--s. 21, ch. 10175, 1925; CGL 8133; s. 384, ch. 71-136; s. 1, ch. 74-128; s. 184, ch. 97-103; s. 1, ch. 2004-287.

Title XXXVIII. Banks and Banking
Chapter 655. Financial Institutions Generally

655.94 Special remedies for nonpayment of rent.—

(1) If the rental due on a safe-deposit box has not been paid for 3 months, the lessor may send a notice by certified mail to the last known address of the lessee stating that the safe-deposit box will be opened and its contents stored at the expense of the lessee unless payment of the rental is made within 30 days. If the rental is not paid within 30 days from the mailing of the notice, the box may be opened in the presence of an officer of the lessor and of a notary public. The contents shall be sealed in a package by a notary public who shall write on the outside the name of the lessee and the date of the opening. The notary public shall execute a certificate reciting the name of the lessee, the date of the opening of the box, and a list of its contents. The certificate shall be included in the package, and a copy of the certificate shall be sent by certified mail to the last known address of the lessee. The package shall then be placed in the general vaults of the lessor at a rental not exceeding the rental previously charged for the box. The lessor has a lien on the package and its contents to the extent of any rental due and owing plus the actual, reasonable costs of removing the contents from the safe-deposit box.

***

History.-- s. 70, ch. 92-303; s. 12, ch. 2004-340; s. 95, ch. 2004-390.

Title XXXIX. Commercial Relations
Chapter 673. Uniform Commercial Code: Negotiable Instruments
Part V. Dishonor

673.5011 Presentment.—

(1) The term "presentment" means a demand made by or on behalf of a person entitled to enforce an instrument:

(a) To pay the instrument made to the drawee or a party obliged to pay the instrument or, in the case of a note or accepted draft payable at a bank, to the bank; or

(b) To accept a draft made to the drawee.

(2) The following rules are subject to chapter 674, agreement of the parties, and clearinghouse rules and the like:

(a) Presentment may be made at the place of payment of the instrument and must be made at the place of payment if the instrument is payable at a bank in the United States; may be made by any commercially reasonable means, including an oral, written, or electronic communication; is effective when the demand for payment or acceptance is received by the person to whom presentment is made; and is effective if made to any one of two or more makers, acceptors, drawees, or other payors.

(b) Upon demand of the person to whom presentment is made, the person making presentment must:

1. Exhibit the instrument;

2. Give reasonable identification and, if presentment is made on behalf of another person, reasonable evidence of authority to do so; and

3. Sign a receipt on the instrument for any payment made or surrender the instrument if full payment is made.

(c) Without dishonoring the instrument, the party to whom presentment is made may:

1. Return the instrument for lack of a necessary indorsement; or

2. Refuse payment or acceptance for failure of the presentment to comply with the terms of the instrument, an agreement of the parties, or other applicable law or rule.

(d) The party to whom presentment is made may treat presentment as occurring on the next business day after the day of presentment if the party to whom presentment is made has established a cutoff hour not earlier than 2 p.m. for the receipt and processing of instruments presented for payment or acceptance and presentment is made after the cutoff hour.

History.—s. 2, ch. 92-82.

673.5021 Dishonor.—

(1) Dishonor of a note is governed by the following rules:

(a) If the note is payable on demand, the note is dishonored if presentment is duly made to the maker and the note is not paid on the day of presentment.

(b) If the note is not payable on demand and is payable at or through a bank or the terms of the note require presentment, the note is dishonored if presentment is duly made and the note is not paid on the day it becomes payable or the day of presentment, whichever is later.

(c) If the note is not payable on demand and paragraph (b) does not apply, the note is dishonored if it is not paid on the day it becomes payable.

(2) Dishonor of an unaccepted draft other than a documentary draft is governed by the following rules:

(a) If a check is duly presented for payment to the payor bank otherwise than for immediate payment over the counter, the check is dishonored if the payor bank:

1. Makes timely return of the check or sends timely notice of dishonor or nonpayment under s. 674.301 or s. 674.302; or

2. Becomes accountable for the amount of the check under s. 674.302.

(b) If a draft is payable on demand and paragraph (a) does not apply, the draft is dishonored if presentment for payment is duly made to the drawee and the draft is not paid on the day of presentment.

(c) If a draft is payable on a date stated in the draft, the draft is dishonored if:

1. Presentment for payment is duly made to the drawee and payment is not made on the day the draft becomes payable or the day of presentment, whichever is later; or

2. Presentment for acceptance is duly made before the day the draft becomes payable and the draft is not accepted on the day of presentment.

(d) If a draft is payable on elapse of a period of time after sight or acceptance, the draft is dishonored if presentment for acceptance is duly made and the draft is not accepted on the day of presentment.

(3) Dishonor of an unaccepted documentary draft occurs according to the rules stated in paragraphs (b), (c), and (d) of subsection (2), except that payment or acceptance may be delayed without dishonor until no later than the close of the third business day of the drawee following the day on which payment or acceptance is required by those paragraphs.

(4) Dishonor of an accepted draft is governed by the following rules:

(a) If the draft is payable on demand, the draft is dishonored if presentment for payment is duly made to the acceptor and the draft is not paid on the day of presentment.

(b) If the draft is not payable on demand, the draft is dishonored if presentment for payment is duly made to the acceptor and payment is not made on the day it becomes payable or the day of presentment, whichever is later.

(5) In any case in which presentment is otherwise required for dishonor under this section and presentment is excused under s. 673.5041, dishonor occurs without presentment if the instrument is not duly accepted or paid.

(6) If a draft is dishonored because timely acceptance of the draft was not made and the person entitled to demand acceptance consents to a late acceptance, from the time of acceptance the draft is treated as never having been dishonored.

History.—s. 2, ch. 92-82.

673.5031 Notice of dishonor.—

(1) The obligation of an indorser stated in s. 673.4151(1) and the obligation of a drawer stated in s. 673.4141(4) may not be enforced unless:

(a) The indorser or drawer is given notice of dishonor of the instrument complying with this section; or

(b) Notice of dishonor is excused under s. 673.5041(2).

(2) Notice of dishonor may be given by any person; may be given by any commercially reasonable means, including an oral, written, or electronic communication; and is sufficient if it reasonably identifies the instrument and indicates that the instrument has been dishonored or has not been paid or accepted. Return of an instrument given to a bank for collection is sufficient notice of dishonor.

(3) Subject to s. 673.5041(3), with respect to an instrument taken for collection by a collecting bank, notice of dishonor must be given by the bank before midnight of the next banking day following the banking day on which the bank receives notice of dishonor of the instrument or by any other person within 30 days following the day on which the person receives notice

of dishonor. With respect to any other instrument, notice of dishonor must be given within 30 days following the day on which dishonor occurs.

History.—s. 2, ch. 92-82.

673.5041 Excused presentment and notice of dishonor.—

(1) Presentment for payment or acceptance of an instrument is excused if:

(a) The person entitled to present the instrument cannot with reasonable diligence make presentment;

(b) The maker or acceptor has repudiated an obligation to pay the instrument or is dead or in insolvency proceedings;

(c) By the terms of the instrument, presentment is not necessary to enforce the obligation of indorsers or the drawer;

(d) The drawer or indorser whose obligation is being enforced has waived presentment or otherwise has no reason to expect or right to require that the instrument be paid or accepted; or

(e) The drawer instructed the drawee not to pay or accept the draft or the drawee was not obligated to the drawer to pay the draft.

(2) Notice of dishonor is excused if, by the terms of the instrument, notice of dishonor is not necessary to enforce the obligation of a party to pay the instrument or if the party whose obligation is being enforced waived notice of dishonor. A waiver of presentment is also a waiver of notice of dishonor.

(3) Delay in giving notice of dishonor is excused if the delay was caused by circumstances beyond the control of the person giving the notice and the person giving the notice exercised reasonable diligence after the cause of the delay ceased to operate.

History.—s. 2, ch. 92-82.

673.5051 Evidence of dishonor.—

(1) The following are admissible as evidence and create a presumption of dishonor and of any notice of dishonor stated:

(a) A document regular in form as provided in subsection (2) which purports to be a protest;

(b) A purported stamp or writing of the drawee, payor bank, or presenting bank on or accompanying the instrument stating that acceptance or payment has been refused unless reasons for the refusal are stated and the reasons are not consistent with dishonor; and

(c) A book or record of the drawee, payor bank, or collecting bank, kept in the usual course of business, which shows dishonor, even if there is no evidence of who made the entry.

(2) A protest is a certificate of dishonor made by a United States consul or vice consul, or a notary public or other person authorized to administer oaths by the law of the place where dishonor occurs. It may be made upon information satisfactory to that person. The protest must identify the instrument and certify that presentment has been made, or, if not made, the reason why it was not made, and that the instrument has been dishonored by nonacceptance or nonpayment. The protest may also certify that notice of dishonor has been given to some or all parties.

History.—s. 2, ch. 92-82.

Title XL. Real and Personal Property
Chapter 695. Record of Conveyances of Real Estate

695.03 Acknowledgment and proof; validation of certain acknowledgments; legalization or authentication before foreign officials.— To entitle any instrument concerning real property to be recorded, the execution must be acknowledged by the party executing it, proved by a subscribing witness to it, or legalized or authenticated by a civil-law notary or notary public who affixes her or his official seal, before the officers and in the form and manner following:

(1) WITHIN THIS STATE.—An acknowledgment or proof made within this state may be made before a judge, clerk, or deputy clerk of any court; a United States commissioner or magistrate; or a notary public or civil-law notary of this state, and the certificate of acknowledgment or proof must be under the seal of the court or officer, as the case may be. All affidavits and acknowledgments heretofore made or taken in this manner are hereby validated.

(2) WITHOUT THIS STATE BUT WITHIN THE UNITED STATES.—An acknowledgment or proof made out of this state but within the United States may be made before a civil-law notary of this state or a commissioner of deeds appointed by the Governor of this state; a judge or clerk of any court of the United States or of any state, territory, or district; a United States commissioner or magistrate; or a notary public, justice of the peace, master in chancery, or registrar or recorder of deeds of any state, territory, or district having a seal, and the certificate of acknowledgment or proof must be under the seal of the court or officer, as the case may be. If the acknowledgment or proof is made before a notary public who does not affix a seal, it is sufficient for the notary public to type, print, or write by hand on the instrument, "I am a Notary Public of the State of (state), and my commission expires on (date)."

(3) WITHIN FOREIGN COUNTRIES.—If the acknowledgment, legalization, authentication, or proof is made in a foreign country, it may be made before a commissioner of deeds appointed by the Governor of this state to act in such country; before a notary public of such foreign country or a civil-law notary of this state or of such foreign country who has an official seal; before an ambassador, envoy extraordinary, minister plenipotentiary, minister, commissioner, charge d'affaires, consul general, consul, vice consul, consular agent, or other diplomatic or consular officer of the United States appointed to reside in such country; or before a military or naval officer authorized by the Laws or Articles of War of the United States to perform the duties of notary public, and the certificate of acknowledgment, legalization, authentication, or proof must be under the seal of the officer. A certificate legalizing or authenticating the signature of a person executing an instrument concerning real property and to which a civil-law notary or notary public of that country has affixed her or his official seal is sufficient as an acknowledgment. For the purposes of this section, the term "civil-law notary" means a civil-law notary as defined in chapter 118 or an official of a foreign country who has an official seal and

who is authorized to make legal or lawful the execution of any document in that jurisdiction, in which jurisdiction the affixing of her or his official seal is deemed proof of the execution of the document or deed in full compliance with the laws of that jurisdiction.

All affidavits, legalizations, authentications, and acknowledgments heretofore made or taken in the manner set forth above are hereby validated.

History.—RS 1973; ch. 5404, 1905; GS 2481; ss. 1, 2, ch. 7849, 1919; RGS 3823; CGL 5699; s. 7, ch. 22858, 1945; s. 1, ch. 28225, 1953; s. 1, ch. 69-79; s. 1, ch. 71-53; s. 26, ch. 73-334; s. 3, ch. 80-173; s. 1, ch. 84-97; s. 763, ch. 97-102; s. 21, ch. 98-246.

695.031 Affidavits and acknowledgments by members of armed forces and their spouses.—

(1) In addition to the manner, form and proof of acknowledgment of instruments as now provided by law, any person serving in or with the Armed Forces of the United States, including the Army, Navy, Marine Corps, Coast Guard, or any component or any arm or service of any thereof, including any female auxiliary of any thereof, and any person whose duties require his or her presence with the Armed Forces of the United States, as herein designated, or otherwise designated by law or military or naval command, may acknowledge any instrument, wherever located, either within or without the state, or without the United States, before any commissioned officer in active service of the Armed Forces of the United States, as herein designated, or otherwise designated by law, or military or naval command, or order, with the rank of second lieutenant or higher in the Army or Marine Corps, or of any component or any arm or service of either thereof, including any female auxiliary of any thereof, or ensign or higher in the Navy or United States Coast Guard, or of any component or any arm or service of either thereof, including any female auxiliary of any thereof.

(2) The instrument shall not be rendered invalid by the failure to state therein the place of execution or acknowledgment. No authentication of the officer's certificate of acknowledgment or otherwise shall be required, and no seal shall be necessary, but the officer taking the acknowledgment shall endorse thereon or attach thereto a certificate substantially in the following form:

On this _____ day of _____, 19_____, before me _____, the undersigned officer, personally appeared _____, known to me (or satisfactorily proven) to be serving in or with, or whose duties require her or his presence with the Armed Forces of the United States, and to be the person whose name is subscribed to the within instrument, and acknowledged that she or he executed the same for the purposes therein contained, and the undersigned does further certify that she or he is at the date of this certificate a commissioned officer of the rank stated below and is in the active service of the Armed Forces of the United States. (Signature of commissioned officer.) (Rank of commissioned officer and command or branch of service to which officer is attached.)

(3) Such acknowledgments by a married woman, who is a member of the Armed Forces of the United States, shall be sufficient in all respects to

bar the dower, homestead rights or separate property rights of such married woman in any real estate described in the instrument thus acknowledged by her, as fully and completely as though such married woman had acknowledged such instrument as now required by other statutes.

(4) An acknowledgment by the spouse of a member of the Armed Forces of the United States shall be sufficient in all respects if it is acknowledged in the manner and form herein provided and shall have the same force and effect as though the instrument had been acknowledged as now required by other statutes and such acknowledgment by a married woman who is a spouse of a member of the Armed Forces of the United States shall be sufficient in all respects to bar the dower, homestead rights or separate property rights of such married woman in any real estate described in the instrument thus acknowledged by her as fully and completely as though such married woman acknowledged such instrument as now required by other statutes.

(5) Any instrument or document acknowledged in the manner and form herein provided shall be entitled to be recorded and shall be recorded as in the case of other instruments or documents properly acknowledged.

(6) This section is to be liberally construed in favor of the validity of any such acknowledgments by any such member of the Armed Forces of the United States and any acknowledgments heretofore taken, containing words of similar import, are hereby confirmed and declared to be valid and binding. This section shall be construed as an enabling act and as an exception to existing laws rather than, inferentially or otherwise, as a repeal of the same or any part of the same.

History.—s. 7, ch. 22858, 1945; s. 1, ch. 57-40; s. 764, ch. 97-102.
Note.—Former s. 120.08.

695.04 Requirements of certificate.— The certificate of the officer before whom the acknowledgment or proof is taken, except for a certificate legalizing or authenticating the signature of a person executing an instrument concerning real property pursuant to s. 695.03(3), shall contain and set forth substantially the matter required to be done or proved to make such acknowledgment or proof effectual.

History.—RS 1974; GS 2482; RGS 3824; CGL 5700; s. 2, ch. 84-97.

695.05 Certain defects cured as to acknowledgments and witnesses.— All deeds, conveyances, bills of sale, mortgages or other transfers of real or personal property within the limits of this state, heretofore or hereafter made and received bona fide and upon good consideration by any corporation, and acknowledged for record before some officer, stockholder or other person interested in the corporation, grantee, or mortgagee as a notary public or other officer authorized to take acknowledgments of instruments for record within this state, shall be held, deemed and taken as valid as if acknowledged by the proper notary public or other officer authorized to take acknowledgments of instruments for record in this state not so interested in said corporation, grantee or mortgagee; and said instrument whenever recorded shall be deemed notice to all persons; provided, however, that this section shall not apply to any instrument heretofore made, the validity of which shall be contested by suit commenced within 1 year of the effective date of this law.

History.—s. 1, ch. 4953, 1901; GS 2483; RGS 3825; s. 1, ch. 11991, 1927; CGL 5701, 5702; s. 1, ch. 14706, 1931; CGL 1936 Supp. 5702(1); s. 11, ch. 20954, 1941.

695.06 Certain irregularities as to venue validated.— Whenever, in the acknowledgment to any deed or other instrument relating to real estate, heretofore recorded in this state, it shall appear, either from the recitals in such acknowledgment, or following the signature of the officer taking the same, or from the seal of such officer that the said acknowledgment was not taken, or may not have been taken, in the place as stated in the caption or venue thereof, said deed or other instrument shall, notwithstanding such irregularity or defect, be deemed and taken as properly acknowledged and of record.

History.—s. 1, ch. 11990, 1927; CGL 5703.

695.09 Identity of grantor.— No acknowledgment or proof shall be taken, except as set forth in s. 695.03(3), by any officer within or without the United States unless the officer knows, or has satisfactory proof, that the person making the acknowledgment is the individual described in, and who executed, such instrument or that the person offering to make proof is one of the subscribing witnesses to such instrument.

History.—RS 1975; GS 2486; RGS 3828; CGL 5706; s. 3, ch. 84-97; s. 765, ch. 97-102.

695.10 Proof by others.— Where the grantors and witnesses of any instrument which may be recorded are dead, or cannot be had, the judge of the circuit court, or the county court judge for the county wherein the real property is situated, may take the examination of any competent witness or witnesses, on oath, to prove the handwriting of the witness or witnesses, or where such proof cannot be had, then to prove the handwriting of the grantor or grantors, which shall be certified by the judge, and the instrument being thus proved may be recorded.

History.—RS 1976; GS 2487; RGS 3829; CGL 5707; s. 26, ch. 73-334.

695.25 Short form of acknowledgment.— The forms of acknowledgment set forth in this section may be used, and are sufficient for their respective purposes, under any law of this state. The forms shall be known as "Statutory Short Forms of Acknowledgment" and may be referred to by that name. The authorization of the forms in this section does not preclude the use of other forms.

(1) For an individual acting in his or her own right:

STATE OF _____
COUNTY OF _____

The foregoing instrument was acknowledged before me this (date) by (name of person acknowledging), who is personally known to me or who has produced (type of identification) as identification.

_____ (Signature of person taking acknowledgment)
_____ (Name typed, printed or stamped)
_____ (Title or rank)
_____ (Serial number, if any)

(2) For a corporation:

STATE OF _____
COUNTY OF _____

The foregoing instrument was acknowledged before me this (date) by (name of officer or agent, title of officer or agent) of (name of corporation acknowledging), a (state or place of incorporation) corporation, on behalf of the corporation. He/she is personally known to me or has produced (type of identification) as identification.

_____ (Signature of person taking acknowledgment)
_____ (Name typed, printed or stamped)
_____ (Title or rank)
_____ (Serial number, if any)

(3) For a partnership:

STATE OF _____
COUNTY OF _____

The foregoing instrument was acknowledged before me this (date) by (name of acknowledging partner or agent), partner (or agent) on behalf of (name of partnership), a partnership. He/she is personally known to me or has produced (type of identification) as identification.

_____ (Signature of person taking acknowledgment)
_____ (Name typed, printed or stamped)
_____ (Title or rank)
_____ (Serial number, if any)

(4) For an individual acting as principal by an attorney-in-fact:

STATE OF _____
COUNTY OF _____

The foregoing instrument was acknowledged before me this (date) by (name of attorney-in-fact) as attorney-in-fact, who is personally known to me or who has produced (type of identification) as identification on behalf of (name of principal).
_____ (Signature of person taking acknowledgment)
_____ (Name typed, printed or stamped)
_____ (Title or rank)
_____ (Serial number, if any)

(5) By any public officer, trustee, or personal representative:

STATE OF _____
COUNTY OF _____
The foregoing instrument was acknowledged before me this (date) by (name and title of position), who is personally known to me or who has produced (type of identification) as identification.

_____ (Signature of person taking acknowledgment)
_____ (Name typed, printed or stamped)
_____ (Title or rank)
_____ (Serial number, if any)

History.—s. 1, ch. 73-62; s. 10, ch. 91-291; s. 7, ch. 93-62; s. 772, ch. 97-102.

695.26 Requirements for recording instruments affecting real property.—

(1) No instrument by which the title to real property or any interest therein is conveyed, assigned, encumbered, or otherwise disposed of shall be recorded by the clerk of the circuit court unless:

(a) The name of each person who executed such instrument is legibly printed, typewritten, or stamped upon such instrument immediately beneath the signature of such person and the post-office address of each such person is legibly printed, typewritten, or stamped upon such instrument;

(b) The name and post-office address of the natural person who prepared the instrument or under whose supervision it was prepared are legibly printed, typewritten, or stamped upon such instrument;

(c) The name of each witness to the instrument is legibly printed, typewritten, or stamped upon such instrument immediately beneath the signature of such witness;

(d) The name of any notary public or other officer authorized to take acknowledgments or proofs whose signature appears upon the instrument is legibly printed, typewritten, or stamped upon such instrument immediately beneath the signature of such notary public or other officer authorized to take acknowledgment or proofs;

(e) A 3-inch by 3-inch space at the top right-hand corner on the first page and a 1-inch by 3-inch space at the top right-hand corner on each subsequent page are reserved for use by the clerk of the court; and

(f) In any instrument other than a mortgage conveying or purporting to convey any interest in real property, the name and post-office address of each grantee in such instrument are legibly printed, typewritten, or stamped upon such instrument.

(2) If a name or address is printed, typewritten, or stamped on an instrument in a position other than the position required by subsection (1), the clerk of the circuit court may, in her or his discretion, accept the instrument for recordation if she or he determines that the connection between the signature and the name or the name and the address is apparent.

(3) This section does not apply to:

(a) An instrument executed before July 1, 1991.

(b) A decree, order, judgment, or writ of any court.

(c) An instrument executed, acknowledged, or proved outside of this state.

(d) A will.

(e) A plat.

(f) An instrument prepared or executed by any public officer other than a notary public.

(4) The failure of the clerk of the circuit court to comply with this section does not impair the validity of the recordation or of the constructive notice imparted by recordation.

History.—s. 1, ch. 90-183; ss. 8, 22, ch. 94-348; s. 773, ch. 97-102.

695.27 Uniform Real Property Electronic Recording Act.—

(1) SHORT TITLE.--This section may be cited as the "Uniform Real Property Electronic Recording Act."

(2) DEFINITIONS.--As used in this section:

(a) "Document" means information that is:

1. Inscribed on a tangible medium or that is stored in an electronic or other medium and is retrievable in perceivable form; and

2. Eligible to be recorded in the Official Records, as defined in s. 28.222, and maintained by a county recorder.

(b) "Electronic" means relating to technology having electrical, digital, magnetic, wireless, optical, electromagnetic, or similar capabilities.

(c) "Electronic document" means a document that is received by a county recorder in an electronic form.

(d) "Electronic signature" means an electronic sound, symbol, or process that is executed or adopted by a person with the intent to sign the document and is attached to or logically associated with a document such that, when recorded, it is assigned the same document number or a consecutive page number immediately following such document.

(e) "Person" means an individual, corporation, business trust, estate, trust, partnership, limited liability company, association, joint venture, public corporation, government or governmental subdivision, agency, instrumentality, or any other legal or commercial entity.

(f) "State" means a state of the United States, the District of Columbia, Puerto Rico, the United States Virgin Islands, or any territory or insular possession subject to the jurisdiction of the United States.

(3) VALIDITY OF ELECTRONIC DOCUMENTS.—

(a) If a law requires, as a condition for recording, that a document be an original, be on paper or another tangible medium, or be in writing, the requirement is satisfied by an electronic document satisfying the requirements of this section.

(b) If a law requires, as a condition for recording, that a document be signed, the requirement is satisfied by an electronic signature.

(c) A requirement that a document or a signature associated with a document be notarized, acknowledged, verified, witnessed, or made under oath is satisfied if the electronic signature of the person authorized to perform that act, and all other information required to be included, is attached to or logically associated with the document or signature. A physical or electronic image of a stamp, impression, or seal need not accompany an electronic signature.

(4) RECORDING OF DOCUMENTS.—

(a) In this subsection, the term "paper document" means a document that is received by the county recorder in a form that is not electronic.

(b) A county recorder:

1. Who implements any of the functions listed in this section shall do so in compliance with standards established by rule by the Department of State.

2. May receive, index, store, archive, and transmit electronic documents.

3. May provide for access to, and for search and retrieval of, documents and information by electronic means.

4. Who accepts electronic documents for recording shall continue to accept paper documents as authorized by state law and shall place entries for both types of documents in the same index.

5. May convert paper documents accepted for recording into electronic form.

6. May convert into electronic form information recorded before the county recorder began to record electronic documents.

7. May agree with other officials of a state or a political subdivision thereof, or of the United States, on procedures or processes to facilitate the electronic satisfaction of prior approvals and conditions precedent to recording.

(5) ADMINISTRATION AND STANDARDS.—

(a) The Department of State, by rule pursuant to ss. 120.536(1) and 120.54, shall prescribe standards to implement this section in consultation with the Electronic Recording Advisory Committee, which is hereby created. The Florida Association of Court Clerks and Comptrollers shall provide administrative support to the committee and technical support to the Department of State and the committee at no charge. The committee shall consist of nine members, as follows:

1. Five members appointed by the Florida Association of Court Clerks and Comptrollers, one of whom must be an official from a large urban charter county where the duty to maintain official records exists in a county office other than the clerk of court or comptroller.

2. One attorney appointed by the Real Property, Probate and Trust Law Section of The Florida Bar Association.

3. Two members appointed by the Florida Land Title Association.

4. One member appointed by the Florida Bankers Association.

(b) Appointed members shall serve a 1-year term. All initial terms shall commence on the effective date of this act. Members shall serve until their successors are appointed. An appointing authority may reappoint a member for successive terms. A vacancy on the committee shall be filled in the same manner in which the original appointment was made, and the term shall be for the balance of the unexpired term.

(c) The first meeting of the committee shall be within 60 days of the effective date of this act. Thereafter, the committee shall meet at the call of the chair, but at least annually.

(d) The members of the committee shall serve without compensation and shall not claim per diem and travel expenses from the Secretary of State.

(e) To keep the standards and practices of county recorders in this state in harmony with the standards and practices of recording offices in other jurisdictions that enact substantially this section and to keep the technology used by county recorders in this state compatible with technology used by recording offices in other jurisdictions that enact substantially this section, the Department of State, in consultation with the committee, so far as is consistent with the purposes, policies, and provisions of this section, in adopting, amending, and repealing standards, shall consider:

1. Standards and practices of other jurisdictions.

2. The most recent standards adopted by national standard-setting bodies, such as the Property Records Industry Association.

3. The views of interested persons and governmental officials and entities.

4. The needs of counties of varying size, population, and resources.

5. Standards requiring adequate information security protection to ensure that electronic documents are accurate, authentic, adequately preserved, and resistant to tampering.

(f) The committee shall terminate on July 1, 2010.

(6) UNIFORMITY OF APPLICATION AND CONSTRUCTION.--In applying and construing this section, consideration must be given to the need to promote uniformity of the law with respect to its subject matter among states that enact it.

(7) RELATION TO ELECTRONIC SIGNATURES IN GLOBAL AND NATIONAL COMMERCE ACT.--This section modifies, limits, and supersedes the federal Electronic Signatures in Global and National Commerce Act, 15 U.S.C. ss. 7001 et seq., but this section does not modify, limit, or supersede s. 101(c) of that act, 15 U.S.C. s. 7001(c), or authorize electronic delivery of any of the notices described in s. 103(b) of that act, 15 U.S.C. s. 7003(b).

Title XLII. Estates and Trusts
Chapter 732. Intestate Succession and Wills
Part V. Wills

732.502 Execution of wills.— Every will must be in writing and executed as follows:

(1)(a) Testator's signature.—

1. The testator must sign the will at the end; or

2. The testator's name must be subscribed at the end of the will by some other person in the testator's presence and by his or her direction.

(b) Witnesses.—The testator's:

1. Signing, or

2. Acknowledgment:

a. That he or she has previously signed the will, or

b. That another person has subscribed the testator's name to it, must be in the presence of at least two attesting witnesses.

(c) Witnesses' signatures.—The attesting witnesses must sign the will in the presence of the testator and in the presence of each other.

(2) Any will, other than a holographic or nuncupative will, executed by a nonresident of Florida, either before or after this law takes effect, is valid as a will in this state if valid under the laws of the state or country where the testator was at the time of execution. A will in the testator's handwriting that has been executed in accordance with subsection (1) shall not be considered a holographic will.

(3) No particular form of words is necessary to the validity of a will if it is executed with the formalities required by law.

(4) A codicil shall be executed with the same formalities as a will.

History.—s. 1, ch. 74-106; s. 21, ch. 75-220; s. 11, ch. 77-87; s. 961, ch. 97-102.

Note.—Created from former s. 731.07.

732.503 Self-proof of will.— A will or codicil executed in conformity with s. 732.502(1) and (2) may be made self-proved at the time of its execution or at any subsequent date by the acknowledgment of it by the testator and the affidavits of the witnesses, each made before an officer authorized to administer oaths and evidenced by the officer's certificate attached to or following the will, in substantially the following form:

STATE OF _____
COUNTY OF _____

We, _____, _____, and _____ the testator and the witnesses, respectively, whose names are signed to the attached or foregoing instrument, having been sworn, declared to the undersigned officer that the testator, in the presence of witnesses, signed the instrument as the testator's last will (codicil), that the testator (signed) (or directed another to sign for him or her), and that each of the witnesses, in the presence of the testator and in the presence of each other, signed the will as a witness.

_____ (Testator)
_____ (Witness)
_____ (Witness)

Subscribed and sworn to before me by _____, the testator who is personally known to me or who has produced (type of identification) as identification, and by _____, a witness who is personally known to me or who has produced (type of identification) as identification, and by _____, a witness who is personally known to me or who has produced (type of identification) as identification, on _____, (year).

_____ (Signature of Notary Public)
(Print, type, or stamp commissioned name of Notary Public)

History.—s. 1, ch. 74-106; s. 21, ch. 75-220; s. 12, ch. 77-87; s. 8, ch. 93-62; s. 962, ch. 97-102; s. 18, ch. 98-246.

Note.—Created from former s. 731.071.

732.504 Who may witness.—

(1) Any person competent to be a witness may act as a witness to a will.

(2) A will or codicil, or any part of either, is not invalid because the will or codicil is signed by an interested witness.

History.—s. 1, ch. 74-106; s. 22, ch. 75-220; s. 1, ch. 77-174; s. 268, ch. 79-400.

Title XLIII. Domestic Relations
Chapter 741. Husband and Wife

741.07 Persons authorized to solemnize matrimony.—
(1) All regularly ordained ministers of the gospel or elders in communion with some church, or other ordained clergy, and all judicial officers, including retired judicial officers, clerks of the circuit courts, and notaries public of this state may solemnize the rights of matrimonial contract, under the regulations prescribed by law. Nothing in this section shall make invalid a marriage which was solemnized by any member of the clergy, or as otherwise provided by law prior to July 1, 1978.
***

History.—s. 1, Nov. 2, 1829; s. 2, ch. 1127, 1861; RS 2056; GS 2575; RGS 3934; CGL 5853; s. 1, ch. 28104, 1953; s. 1, ch. 74-372; s. 1, ch. 78-15; s. 34, ch. 95-401.

741.08 Marriage not to be solemnized without a license.— Before any of the persons named in s. 741.07 shall solemnize any marriage, he or she shall require of the parties a marriage license issued according to the requirements of s. 741.01, and within 10 days after solemnizing the marriage he or she shall make a certificate thereof on the license, and shall transmit the same to the office of the county court judge or clerk of the circuit court from which it issued.

History.—ss. 2, 3, Nov. 2, 1829; s. 1, ch. 3890, 1889; RS 2057; GS 2576; RGS 3935; CGL 5854; s. 28, ch. 73-334; s. 1, ch. 74-372; s. 1059, ch. 97-102.

741.10 Proof of marriage where no certificate available.— When any marriage is or has been solemnized by any of the persons named in s. 741.07, and such person has not made a certificate thereof on the marriage license as required by s. 741.08, or when the marriage license has been lost, or when by reason of death or other cause the proper certificate cannot be obtained, the marriage may be proved by affidavit before any officer authorized to administer oaths made by two competent witnesses who were present and saw the marriage ceremony performed, which affidavit may be filed and recorded in the office of the county court judge or clerk of the circuit court from which the marriage license issued, with the same force and effect as in cases in which the proper certificate has been made, returned and recorded.

History.--s. 1, ch. 3126, 1879; RS 2059; GS 2578; RGS 3937; CGL 5856; s. 28, ch. 73-334; s. 1, ch. 74-372.

Title XLVI. Crimes
Chapter 839. Offenses by Public Officers and Employees

838.022 Official misconduct.—
(1) It is unlawful for a public servant, with corrupt intent to obtain a benefit for any person or to cause harm to another, to:
(a) Falsify, or cause another person to falsify, any official record or official document;
(b) Conceal, cover up, destroy, mutilate, or alter any official record or official document or cause another person to perform such an act; or

(c) Obstruct, delay, or prevent the communication of information relating to the commission of a felony that directly involves or affects the public agency or public entity served by the public servant.

(2) For the purposes of this section:

(a) The term "public servant" does not include a candidate who does not otherwise qualify as a public servant.

(b) An official record or official document includes only public records.

(3) Any person who violates this section commits a felony of the third degree, punishable as provided in s. 775.082, s. 775.083, or s. 775.084.

History.--s. 5, ch. 2003-158.

Florida Administrative Code
Chapter 1, Department of State
Chapter 1N, Division of Corporations
Chapter 1N-5, Electronic Notarization

1N-5.001 Definitions.

(1) "Capable of independent verification" means any interested person may reasonably determine the notary's identity, the notary's relevant authority and that the electronic signature is the act of the particular notary identified by the signature.

(2) "Electronic document" means information that is created, generated, sent, communicated, received, or stored by electronic means.

(3) "Electronic notarization" and "electronic notarial act" means an official act authorized under Section 117.021(1), F.S., using electronic documents and electronic signatures.

(4) "Electronic Notary System" means a set of applications, programs, hardware, software, or technology designed to enable a notary to perform electronic notarizations.

(5) "Electronic signature" means an electronic sound, symbol, or process attached to or logically associated with an electronic document and executed or adopted by a person with the intent to sign the electronic document or record.

(6) "Attached to or logically associated with" means the notary's electronic signature is securely bound to the electronic document in such a manner as to make it impracticable to falsify or alter, without detection, either the signature or the document.

(7) "Unique to the notary public" means the notary's electronic signature is attributable solely to the notary public to the exclusion of all other persons.

(8) "Retained under the notary public's sole control" means accessible by and attributable solely to the notary to the exclusion of all other persons and entities, either through being in the direct physical custody of the notary or through being secured with one or more biometric, password, token, or other authentication technologies in an electronic notarization system that meets the performance requirements of Sections 117.021(2) and (3), F.S.

(9) "Public key certificate" means a computer-based record that:

(a) Identifies the certification authority issuing it;

(b) Names or identifies its subscriber;

(c) Contains the subscriber's public key; and

(d) Is digitally signed by the certification authority issuing it.

Rulemaking Authority 117.021(5) FS. Law Implemented 117.021 FS. History–New 1-26-10.

1N-5.002 Notary's Electronic Signature.

(1) In performing an electronic notarial act, a notary shall execute an electronic signature in a manner that attributes such signature to the notary public identified on the official commission.

(2) A notary shall take reasonable steps to ensure the security, reliability and uniformity of electronic notarizations, including, but not limited to, the use of an authentication procedure such as a password, token, card or biometric to protect access to the notary's electronic signature or the means for affixing the signature.

(3) The notary's electronic signature and seal information may be affixed by means of a public key certificate.

(4) The notary's electronic signature and seal information may be affixed by means of an electronic notary system.

(5) Any public key certificate or electronic notary system that is used to affix the Notary's electronic signature and seal information shall be issued at the third or higher level of assurance as defined by the U. S. National Institute of Standards and Technology (NIST) Special Publication 800-63 (NIST800-63), Electronic Authentication Guideline Version 1.0.2., available at NIST's website www.csrc.nist.gov which may be accessed at the following URL: http://csrc.nist.gov/publications/nistpubs/800-63/SP800-63V1_0_2.pdf.

Rulemaking Authority 117.021(5) FS. Law Implemented 117.021 FS. History–New 1-26-10 ■

Sample Ceremony in Spanish / Ejemplo de Ceremonia en Español

El notario formula: "Queridos amigos aquí presentes, nos hemos reunido hoy (o esta noche) para unir a este hombre y a esta mujer en (sagrado) matrimonio."

Intercambio de votos matrimoniales

El notario le pregunta al hombre: "¿(Nombre del novio) recibe usted a esta mujer para ser su esposa, para vivir juntos en (sagrado) matrimonio, para amarla, honrarla, consolarla y cuidarla, en salud y en enfermedad, guardándole fidelidad, durante el tiempo que duren sus vidas?"

El hombre responde: "Sí quiero."

El notario le pregunta a la mujer: "¿(Nombre de la novia) recibe usted a este hombre para ser su esposo, para vivir juntos en (sagrado) matrimonio, para amarlo, honrarlo, consolarlo y cuidarlo, en salud y en enfermedad, guardándole fidelidad, durante el tiempo que duren sus vidas?"

La mujer responde: "Sí quiero."

El notario formula: "Repita después de mí."

Al hombre: "Yo (nombre del contrayente), te recibo a ti (nombre de la contrayente) para ser mi esposa, para tenerte y protegerte de hoy en adelante, para bien y para mal, en la riqueza y en la pobreza, en salud y en enfermedad, para amarte y cuidarte hasta que la muerte nos separe."

El notario formula: "Repita después de mí."

A la mujer: "Yo (nombre de la contrayente), te recibo a ti (nombre del contrayente) para ser mi esposo, para tenerte y protegerte de hoy en adelante, para bien y para mal, en la riqueza y en la pobreza, en salud y en enfermedad, para amarte y cuidarte hasta que la muerte nos separe."

Intercambio de alianzas matrimoniales (anillos)

El notario le pide al hombre que ponga la alianza en el dedo de la mujer y que repita lo siguiente: "Yo te coloco esta alianza como señal y promesa de nuestro amor constante y fidelidad duradera." (El notario repite lo mismo para la mujer).

Declaración

El notario le pide a la pareja que se tomen de las manos y declara: "En virtud de la autoridad que me conceden las leyes del Estado de la Florida, los declaro marido y mujer."

Offices of Florida Notary Regulating Officials

Notary Commissions:

Department of State
Division of Corporations
Notary Commissions
P.O. Box 6327
Tallahassee, FL 32314
(850) 245-6975

Walk-in Service:

Department of State
Division of Corporations
Notary Commissions or
Apostille Certification
Clifton Building
2661 Executive Center Circle
Tallahassee, FL 32301

Authentications:

Department of State
Division of Corporations
Apostille Certification
P.O. Box 6800
Tallahassee, FL 32314
(850) 245-6945

Governor:

Executive Office of Governor
Notary Section
LL06, The Capitol
Tallahassee, FL 32399-0001
(850) 922-6400

In addition, the Florida Department of State offers walk-in and courier delivery service for authentication:

Department of State
Division of Corporations
Clifton Building
2661 Executive Center Circle
Tallahassee, FL 32301

Additional online resources: *www.dos.state.fl.us* and *www. myflorida.com/myflorida/government/governorinitiatives/notary/ index.html*

Bureaus
of Vital
Statistics

Florida Notaries are not permitted to make certified copies of vital or public records. Persons requesting "notarization" or certified copies of birth or death certificates should be referred to the appropriate public office. The following agencies can provide certified copies of vital records for persons who were born or have died in the respective states. Persons requiring copies of foreign records should contact the appropriate consulate in the U.S.

Alabama
Vital Records
Department of Public Health
P.O. Box 5625
Montgomery, AL 36103-5625

Alaska
Bureau of Vital Statistics
Department of Health &
Social Services
5441 Commercial Blvd.
P.O. Box 110675
Juneau, AK 99801

Arizona
Office of Vital Records
Department of Health Services
P.O. Box 3887
Phoenix, AZ 85030-3887

Arkansas
Division of Vital Records
Department of Health
4815 West Markham Street, Slot 44
Little Rock, AR 72205-3867

California
Office of Vital Records
Department of Health Services
P.O. Box 997410, MS: 5103
Sacramento, CA 95899-7410

Colorado
Vital Records Section
Department of Health
4300 Cherry Creek Drive South
Denver, CO 80246-1530

Connecticut
Department of Public Health
State Office of Vital Records
410 Capitol Avenue, MS #11VRS
P.O. Box 340308
Hartford, CT 06134-0308

Delaware
Health Statistics Center
Office of Vital Statistics
Jesse S. Cooper Building
417 Federal Street
Dover, DE 19901

District of Columbia
Vital Records Division
825 North Capitol Street NE
1st Floor
Washington, DC 20002

Florida
Office of Vital Statistics
1217 Pearl Street
P.O. Box 210
Jacksonville, FL 32231

Georgia
Vital Records
2600 Skyland Drive NE
Atlanta, GA 30319-3640

Hawaii
Vital Statistics Section
State Department of Health
P.O. Box 3378
Honolulu, HI 96801

Idaho
Vital Statistics Unit
450 West State Street, 1st Floor
P.O. Box 83720
Boise, ID 83720-0036

Illinois
Division of Vital Records
Department of Public Health
605 West Jefferson Street
Springfield, IL 62702-5097

Indiana
Vital Records Department
State Department of Health
6 West Washington Street
Indianapolis, IN 46204

Iowa
Department of Public Health
Bureau of Vital Records
Lucas Office Building, 1st Floor
321 East 12th Street
Des Moines, IA 50319-0075

Kansas
Office of Vital Statistics
1000 SW Jackson Street, Suite 120
Topeka, KS 66612-2221

Kentucky
Office of Vital Statistics
Department for Health Services
275 East Main Street, 1E-A
Frankfort, KY 40621-0001

Louisiana
Vital Records Registry
P.O. Box 60630
New Orleans, LA 70160

Maine
Vital Statistics
221 State Street
11 State House Station
Augusta, ME 04333-0011

Maryland
Division of Vital Records
Department of Health
6550 Reisterstown Road
Baltimore, MD 21215

Massachusetts
Registry of Vital Records and
Statistics
150 Mount Vernon St., 1st Floor
Dorchester, MA 02125-3105

Michigan
Vital Records Request
P.O. Box 30721
Lansing, MI 48909

Minnesota
Department of Health
Office of the State Registrar
P.O. Box 64882
St. Paul, MN 55164-0882

Mississippi
Vital Records
P.O. Box 1700
Jackson, MS 39215-1700

Missouri
Department of Health
Bureau of Vital Records
930 Wildwood
P.O. Box 570
Jefferson City, MO 65102-0570

Montana
Office of Vital Statistics
P.O. Box 4210
111 North Sanders, Room 209
Helena, MT 59604

Nebraska
Vital Statistics
Department of Health
301 Centennial Mall South
P.O. Box 95065
Lincoln, NE 68509-5065

Nevada
Office of Vital Records
4150 Technology Way, Suite 104
Carson City, NV 89706

New Hampshire
Department of State
Division of Vital Records
Administration
71 South Fruit Street
Concord, NH 03301-2410

New Jersey
Vital Statistics
Customer Service
P.O. Box 370
Trenton, NJ 08625-0370

New Mexico
Vital Records and Health Statistics
1105 St. Francis Drive
Santa Fe, NM 87502

New York
State Department of Health
Vital Records Section
Certification Unit
P.O. Box 2602
Albany, NY 12220-2602

New York City
Office of Vital Records
New York City Department
of Health
125 Worth Street, CN4, Room 133
New York, NY 10013

North Carolina
Vital Records
1903 Mail Service Center
Raleigh, NC 27699-1903

North Dakota
Division of Vital Records
600 East Boulevard Avenue
Dept. 301
Bismarck, ND 58505-0200

Ohio
Department of Health
Vital Statistics
P.O. Box 15098
Columbus, OH 43215-0098

Oklahoma
Vital Records Service
State Department of Health
1000 Northeast 10th Street
Oklahoma City, OK 73117

Oregon
Vital Records
P.O. Box 14050
Portland, OR 97293-0050

Pennsylvania
Division of Vital Records
101 South Mercer Street
Room 401
P.O. Box 1528
New Castle, PA 16101

Rhode Island
Office of Vital Records
Department of Health
3 Capitol Hill Road, Room 101
Providence, RI 02908-5097

South Carolina
Office of Vital Records
South Carolina DHEC
2600 Bull Street
Columbia, SC 29201

South Dakota
Vital Records
207 East Missouri Avenue
Suite #1A
Pierre, SD 57501

Tennessee
Vital Records
Central Services Building
421 5th Avenue North
Nashville, TN 37247

Texas
Bureau of Vital Statistics
Department of Health
P.O. Box 12040
Austin, TX 78711-2040

Utah
Vital Records and Statistics
Cannon Health Building
288 North 1460 West
P.O. Box 141012
Salt Lake City, UT 84114-1012

Vermont
Department of Health
Vital Records Section
108 Cherry Street
P.O. Box 70
Burlington, VT 05402-0070

Virginia
Office of Vital Records
P.O. Box 1000
Richmond, VA 23218-1000

Washington
Department of Health
Center for Health Statistics
P.O. Box 9709
Olympia, WA 98507-9709

West Virginia
Vital Registration Office
350 Capitol Street, Room 165
Charleston, WV 25301-3701

Wisconsin
Vital Records
1 West Wilson Street
P.O. Box 309
Madison, WI 53701-0309

Wyoming
Vital Records Services
Hathaway Building
Cheyenne, WY 82002

American Samoa
Office of Records and Vital
Statistics
LBJ Tropical Medical Center
Department of Health Services
American Samoa Government
Pago Pago, AS 96799

Guam
Office of Vital Statistics
Department of Public Health
P.O. Box 2816
Agana, GU, M.I. 96910

Northern Mariana Islands
Bureau of Health Planning
Statistics Office
P.O. Box 500409 CK
Saipan, MP 96950-0409

Panama Canal Zone
Vital Records Section
Passport Services
U.S. Department of State
1111 19th Street NW, Suite 510
Washington, DC 20522-1705

Puerto Rico
Department of Health
Demographic Registry
P.O. Box 11854
Fernández Juncos Station
San Juan, PR 00910

Virgin Islands (St. Croix)
Department of Health
Vital Statistics
Charles Harwood Memorial
Hospital
St. Croix, VI 00820

**Virgin Islands
(St. Thomas, St. John)**
Department of Health
Registrar of Vital Statistics
Knud Hansen Complex
St. Thomas, VI 0080

Hague Convention Nations

The nations listed on the following pages are parties to a treaty called the *Hague Convention Abolishing the Requirement of Legalization for Foreign Public Documents*, hereafter simply called the Hague Convention.

Treaty Simplifies Authentication. A Notary's signature on documents that are sent to these nations may be authenticated (verified as valid for the benefit of the recipient in the foreign nation) through attachment of a single authenticating certificate called an *apostille*. The *apostille* (French for "notation") is the only authenticating certificate necessary. Nations not subscribing to the Hague Convention may require as many as five or six separate authenticating certificates from different governmental agencies, domestic and foreign.

How to Request an *Apostille*. To obtain an *apostille*, anyone may mail the notarized document, a self-addressed stamped envelope and a $10 check payable to the "Department of State" to:

> Department of State
> Division of Corporations
> P.O. Box 6800
> Tallahassee, FL 32314-6800
> (850) 245-6945

An *apostille* must be specifically requested, and the nation to which the document will be sent must be indicated. It is not the Notary's responsibility to obtain an *apostille*; it is the responsibility of the party needing authentication.

Hague Convention Nations. The nations listed below participate in the Hague Convention. Footnotes reflect information most likely to be of interest to Notaries acting in the United States and its territories. Please note that some nations listed may not recognize the participation of every other nation listed. To verify recognition between nations, consult the Web site of the Hague Conference on Private International Law at http://www.hcch.net/index_en.php.

Albania	Dominican Republic[13]
Andorra[13]	Ecuador
Antigua and Barbuda[13]	El Salvador[13]
Argentina[1]	Estonia
Armenia[13]	Fiji[13]
Australia	Finland
Austria	France[4]
Azerbaijan[13]	Georgia[5]
Bahamas[13]	Germany[8]
Barbados[13]	Greece
Belarus	Grenada[13]
Belgium[8]	Honduras[13]
Belize[13]	Hong Kong[6]
Bosnia and Herzegovina[2]	Hungary
Botswana[13]	Iceland
Brunei Darussalam[13]	India
Bulgaria	Ireland
Cape Verde[13]	Israel
Colombia[13]	Italy
Cook Islands[13]	Japan
Croatia[2]	Kazakhstan[13]
Cyprus	Latvia
Czech Republic	Lesotho[13]
Denmark[3]	Liberia[8,13]
Dominica[13]	Liechtenstein[13]

1. Argentina does not recognize the extension of the Convention by the United Kingdom to the Malvinas (Falkland Islands), South Georgia, South Sandwich Islands and the Argentine Antarctic Sector (British Antarctic Territory). See n. 11.

2. The former Socialist Federal Republic of Yugoslavia was a party to the Convention. Only the successor states of Bosnia and Herzegovina, Croatia, the Republic of Macedonia, Montenegro, Serbia and Slovenia have confirmed that the Convention still applies.

3. The participation of Denmark does not extend to Greenland and the Faro Islands.

4. The participation of France is extended to the entire territory of the French Republic, including French Guyana, French Polynesia, Guadeloupe, Martinique, Mayotte, New Caledonia, Reunion, St. Barthelemy, St. Martin, St. Pierre and Miquelon, and Wallis and Futuna.

5. The participation of Georgia does not extend to Abkhazia and South Ossetia.

6. Hong Kong and Macao retained their status as Hague nations after control was returned to China on July 1, 1997 (Hong Kong) and December 20, 1999 (Macao).

7. The participation of New Zealand does not extend to Tokelau.

Lithuania
Luxembourg
Macao[6]
Macedonia[2]
Malawi[13]
Malta
Marshall Islands[13]
Mauritius[13]
Mexico
Moldova[13]
Monaco
Mongolia[13]
Montenegro[2]
Namibia[13]
Netherlands[9]
New Zealand[7]
Niue[13]
Norway
Panama
Peru
Poland
Portugal[10]
Romania
Russian Federation
Saint Kitts and Nevis[13]

Saint Lucia[13]
Saint Vincent and the
  Grenadines[13]
Samoa[13]
San Marino[13]
Sao Tome e Principe[13]
Serbia[2]
Seychelles[13]
Slovakia
Slovenia[2]
South Africa
South Korea
Spain
Suriname
Swaziland[13]
Sweden
Switzerland
Tonga[13]
Trinidad and Tobago[13]
Turkey
Ukraine
United Kingdom[1,11]
United States[8,12]
Vanuatu[13]
Venezuela

Inquiries. Persons having questions about the *Hague Convention Abolishing the Requirement of Legalization for Foreign Public Documents* may address their inquiries to:

U.S. Dept. of State
Authentication Office
518 23rd Street, NW
State Annex 1
Washington, DC 20520
(202) 647-5002

---

8. The Convention does not apply between Liberia and the United States, Belgium or Germany.

9. The participation of the Netherlands is extended to Aruba and the Netherlands Antilles.

10. The participation of Portugal is extended to the entire territory of the Republic of Portugal, including the Azores and Madeira.

11. The participation of the United Kingdom of Great Britain and Northern Ireland is extended to Anguilla, Bermuda, British Antarctic Territory, British Virgin Islands, Cayman Islands, Falkland Islands, Gibraltar, Guernsey, Isle of Man, Jersey, Montserrat, St. Helena and Turks and Caicos Islands.

12. The United States includes American Samoa, District of Columbia, Guam, Northern Mariana Islands, Puerto Rico and U.S. Virgin Islands.

13. This nation is not a member of the Hague Conference on Private International Law but is a party to the *Hague Convention Abolishing the Requirement of Legalization for Foreign Public Documents.*

About the NNA

Since 1957, the National Notary Association — a nonprofit educational organization — has served the nation's Notaries Public with a wide variety of instructional programs and services.

As the country's clearinghouse for information on Notary laws, customs and practices, the NNA educates Notaries through publications, seminars, webinars, online training, annual conferences, its website and the NNA Hotline that offers immediate answers to specific questions about notarization.

The Association is perhaps most widely known as the preeminent source of information for and about Notaries. NNA works include the following:

- *The National Notary*, a magazine for NNA members featuring how-to articles and practical tips on notarizing

- *Notary Bulletin*, an online newsletter that keeps NNA members and customers up to date on developments affecting Notaries, especially new state laws and regulations

- *Sorry, No Can Do!* series, four volumes that help Notaries explain to customers and bosses why some requests for notarizations are improper and cannot be accommodated

- *U.S. Notary Reference Manual*, an invaluable resource for any person relying upon the authenticity and correctness of legal documents

- *Notary Public Practices & Glossary*, a definitive reference book on notarial procedures and widely hailed as the Notary's bible

- State *Notary Law Primers*, short guidebooks that explain a state's Notary statutes in easy-to-understand language

- *The Notary Public Code of Professional Responsibility*, a comprehensive and detailed code of ethical and professional conduct for Notaries

- *The Model Notary Act*, prototype legislation conceived in 1973 and updated in 1984, 2002 and 2010 by an NNA-recruited panel of secretaries of state, legislators and attorneys, and regularly used by state legislatures in revising their Notary laws

- *Notary Signing Agent Training Course*, a manual covering every aspect of signing agent procedures that prepares candidates for the Notary Signing Agent Certification Examination developed by the NNA

- Public-service pamphlets informing the general public about the function of a Notary, including *What Is A Notary Public?* printed in English and Spanish

In addition, the NNA offers the highest quality professional supplies, including official seals and stamps, embossers, recordkeeping journals, jurat stamps, thumbprinting devices and notarial certificates.

Though dedicated primarily to educating and assisting Notaries, the NNA supports implementing effective Notary laws and informing the public about the Notary's vital role in modern society. ■

Index

A

Absentee ballot, witnessing ... *84–85*
Acknowledgments 21, **23–27**, *84*
          88–90
    Certificates for **23–26**, 44–46
          59–60, *85, 88–90, 104–105*
          106–108
    Common act 23
    Fee **49**, *84*
    Identification of signer 23, 26
          38–43, *85–87*
    Incomplete documents, of 13
          22, **50**, *93*
    Military officers, by 28, **59–60**
          104–105
    Out of state 27, *103*
    Outside of United States 27
          103–104
    Purpose 23
    Requirements 23, *85–86*
    Short-form certificates **24–26**
          106–107
    Terminology 27
    Who may take 26–27, *103*
    Witnessing signature 26
Address, change of 20, 64, *82–83*
          87
Advertising 57–58, *87*
    False or misleading 57, 66
    Foreign-language 57, **87**
Advice 15, **52**, 57, 60, 66, *87*

Affidavit of domicile *94*
Affidavit of good character 4
          16–17, 47, 82, 84
Affidavit of proof 37
Affidavit of support 58
Affidavits 6–7, 31, 35–38, 58
          61–63, *98, 103–104, 112*
    Certificate for 62
    Oath (Affirmation) for 62
    Procedure 62
    Purpose 61
    Response required 62
Affirmations 22, 31–32, **34–36**
    Affidavit, for 35, 62
    Ceremony 36
    Certificate for *88*
    Credible identifying witnesses,
        for 8, 35
    Deposition, for 63
    Fee 49, *84*
    Gestures 36
    Jurat, for 31
    Power to administer 34, *84*
    Purpose 34
    Response required 36, 62
    Witness in court, for 35
    Wording for 35
Apostilles **56–57**, *96–97*
    Authentication 56–57
    Fee 57, *96*

Page numbers listed in **bold** indicate where the most complete information on a subject can be found. *Italics* indicate the pages where the statutes pertaining to a subject are located.

Out of country 56–57
Procedure.............. 57, *96–97*, 122
Application, commission.......... 4, **16**
82–83
Affidavit of good character 4
16–17
Criminal record................... 17, *82*
Fee.................................... 4, 17, *82*
Fictitious name .. 4, **17**, 64, *82–83*
Misconduct................................64
Misstatement on............. 17, *82–83*
Permanent resident......... 4, 17, *82*
Previous convictions 17, *82*
Residency...............................17, 82
Restoration of civil rights 17
Attested copies. *See* **Certified copies**
Attorney in fact.............24, 26, 36, 44
Certificate for 24, 26
Short-form certificate for...........26
Authentication............. **56–57**, *91–92*
Apostilles............................**56–57**
Hague Convention
nations.......................... 122–124
Out of country 56
Out of state 56
Procedure...........................56–57
Authenticity, certificate of.......56–57
Authority, certificate of............56–57
Authorized Acts 21–22

B

Beneficial interest..........8, **11**, 22, 41
50–51, 65, *86, 93*
Exceptions...................................51
Birth certificates, notarizing.
See **Vital records, notarizing**
Blank certificates, signing 22
46–47, 66
Blanks in documents........ 13, 50, *93*
Blind, notarizing for 55, *89*
Bond, Notary 4, **17–18**, 83, *95*
Claims against......................17–18
Failure to maintain 64
Filing 17, 82, 83
Liability...............................18, 82
Protects Public 18
Requirement..............................17
Surety 17, 82

Bureaus of Vital Statistics 118–121

C

Capacity, certificate of.
See **Authentication**
Certificate, false 66, *114*
Certificate of proof 37
Certificates, notarial....... 6, 23–26, *85*
88–90
Acknowledgments, for .. 23–26, *85*
88–89
Attorney in fact, for 24
Blank......................22, **47**, 66, *92*
Certified copies, for............ 29, *88*
Certified copy of notarial
record, for 29–30
Choosing.....................**14–15**, 46
Contents of.....................45–46, 85
Corporate acknowledgment,
for 24, *88*
Corporation, for.........................88
Correcting 47, 67, *92, 113*
Depositions, for 63
Directs Notary to sign, notarizing
for a person who.......54–55, *90*
Disabled person, for............ 54–55
89–90
False certificate 47, *113*
Inventorying a safe-deposit box,
for 30, *99*
Jurats, for............................. 31, *88*
Loose certificates 45, **46–47**
Marriage, for 34
Military officer notarizations,
for 59–60
Oath or affirmation, for............ *88*
Pre-signed or pre-sealed 47
Representative acknowledgment,
for 24, *88–89*
Seal of Notary 45
Self-proving wills, for 60
111–112
Short-form acknowledgments,
for 24–26
Short forms 24
Signature by mark, for 52, **88**
89–90
Statement of particulars.............45

Testimonium clause....................45
Venue **45**
Wills, for....................60, *111–112*
Certificates, short-form............ 24–26
106–107
Attorney in fact, for 26
Corporate acknowledgment,
for 25
Individual acknowledgment,
for 25–26
Partnership acknowledgment,
for 25
Representative acknowledgment,
for 26
Certification authorities. *See* **Digital signatures**
Certified copies......10, 22, 28–29, *88*
Certificate for 29, *88*
Fees 49
Notarial records, of....................29
Precautions 28–29
Procedure..................................28
Purpose 28
Recordable documents,of 28
Vital records, of 10
Civil-law Notaries 19–20, *94–95*
Authority 19, *94–95*
Jurisdiction 19, *94–95*
Protocol required.......... 19, *94–95*
Qualifications............... 19, *94–95*
Regulations 20, *94–95*
Civil penalties. *See* **Misconduct**
College diplomas, notarizing 10
Commission, Notary................16–21
Address, change of............. 20, *83*
Amended.............................20, 83
Commission application..............3
Renewal of...................................3
Resignation of.....................20–21
Suspension of 20
Conformed copy............................9
Course on notarization...................4
Credible identifying witness 8
38–43
Identification of 40

Not a subscribing witness ... 42–43
Oath (affirmation) for...............40
Purpose 40
Qualifications.............................40
Signature in Notary's journal.....42
Written statement for...........41–42
Criminal record.......................21, 82
Customers, restricting services
to 9–10

D

Death records 10
Depositions............................**62–64**
Certificate for 63
Oath (affirmation) for..........63–64
Procedure...................................62
Purpose **62–63**
Response required.....................63
Digital signatures. *See* **Electronic signatures**
Directing Notary to sign....53–54, *90*
Certificates for...............53–54, *90*
Identification of principal... 54, *90*
Journal entry...............................55
Persons with a disability 53, *90*
Procedure........................... 54, *90*
Disqualifying interest......... 22–23, 41
50–51, 65, *86, 93*
Exceptions...................................51
Notarizing for relatives ..**11**, 23, *86*
Documents
Authentication of.......................56
Blank spaces, with 13, **50**, *93*
Date, checking...........................14
Date of 14
Foreign language.......................58
Immigration 58, *87*
Incomplete..................13, **50**, *93*
Preparation of.....................15, 52
Scanning of 13
Selection of 15, 52
Sent out of country...................56
Sent out of state..................56–57

Page numbers listed in **bold** indicate where the most complete information on a subject can be found. *Italics* indicate the pages where the statutes pertaining to a subject are located.

E

Education, Notary 4
Electronic notarizations 68–71, *91*
             96–100, 114–115
   Administrative rules 69, *91*
   Attribution 71, *114*
   Authority to perform *91*
   Certificate for electronic
      notarization 73–74
   Certificates *96*
   Certification authority *96*
   Earlier act repealed *93*
   Legislative enactments 68–69
   Physical presence required 73
Electronic Notary system 73, *114*
Electronic record 69
Electronic signatures 69–70, *91*
              96–97, 115
   Public key certificate 72–73, *96*
              114–115
   Seal information 74
Embosser seal 5, *85*
Employer liability 68
Equipment, notarial 5–6
Errors and omissions insurance 6
Exam, practice 75–80

F

Facsimile signature, Notary 67
False names, signing 66
Family members, notarizing for **11**
              23, 65, *93*
Fees 49–50, *84*
   Absentee ballots, for 50, *84*
   Acknowledgments, for 49
   Affirmations, for 49
   Application **4**, 17, 82
   Certified copy, for 49
   Inventorying a safe-deposit box,
      for 49
   Jurats, for 49
   Marriage, for 49
   Maximum 49, *84*
   Oaths, for 49
   Option not to charge 49
   Overcharging 50, *84*
   Travel 50

Verifying a vehicle identification
   number, for 49
Financial interest **11**, 41, **50–51**
             65, *86, 93*
   Exceptions 51
Fines. *See* **Misconduct**
Fingerprinting device 6
Flags. *See* **Authentication**
Florida Administrative
   Code *114–115*
   1N-5.001 .... 71–73, *114–115*
   1N-5.002 .... 71–73, *115*
Florida Statutes
   28.24 .... 34, 49, *93–94*
   28.24[29] 34
   117.01 .... 16–21, 50, 57, 64–68
              82–84
   117.03 .... 22, 34–35, 67, *84*
   117.04 .... 21, 32, 34, 49, *84*
   117.05 .... 21–23, 26–29, 31–32
       38–40, 42, 44, 46–50, 52–54
        57–58, 64–68, *84–91*
   117.06 .... *91*
   117.10 .... 19, *91*
   117.20 .... 18, *93*
   117.021 .... *91*
   117.045 .... 21, 32, 34, 49, *84*
   117.103 .... 56, *91–92*
   117.105 .... 47, 66, 93
   117.107 .... 22–23, 47–48, 50, 58
          65–68, *92–93*
   117.108 .... *93*
   118.10 .... 19, *94–95*
   118.12 .... *96–97*
   319.23 .... 22, 37, *98*
   454.23 .... 52, 66, *98*
   655.94 .... 21, 30, *99*
   668.50 .... 16, *97*
   673.5011 .... *99*
   673.5021 .... *100–101*
   673.5031 .... *101–102*
   673.5041 .... *101, 102*
   673.5051 .... *102*
   695.03 ...... 22, 27, 37, 59, *103–105*
   695.04 .... *105*
   695.05 .... *105–106*
   695.06 .... *106*
   695.09 .... *106*

695.10 .... *106*
695.25 .... 24, 27, *106*
695.26 .... *108*
695.27 ....*104–107*
695.031 ....*104–105*
732.502 .... *111*
732.503 .... 60, *112*
732.504 .... 61, *112*
741.07 .... 32, *113*
741.08 .... 34, *113*
741.10 .... *113*
742.07 ....*32*
838.022 ....65, *83*, *113*
6681 .... *96*
6682 .... *96*
6683 .... *96*
6684 .... *97*
6686 .... *97*
Foreign language 10, **58–59**, *87*
    Advertising 57–58, *87*
    Documents......................10, 58, 67
    Signers **58–59**, 67, *92*

G
Governor, office of 82, 117
Governor's Reference Manual for
    Notaries (RMN) 10, 14, 16, 22
                    30, 32–33, 37, 38, 41, 43
                    48, 51, 60, 63

H
Hague...122
Hague Convention Abolishing the
    Requirement of Legalization for
    Foreign Public Documents........57
                    122–124
Hague Convention
    Nations 122–124
How to Become a Florida
    Notary..3–4

I
Identification.......... 8, 12, **38–43**, *86*
    Credible identifying
        witness......................38–43, *86*

Documents.....................39–40, *86*
Immigration documents 39, *86*
Indicate on certificate... 38, 42, *86*
Minors of......................................56
Personal knowledge................. *86*
Procedure.....................................38
Satisfactory evidence *86*
Vehicle.....................................37–38
Identification documents...39–40, *86*
    Acceptable 39–40, *86*
    Multiple 40
    Unacceptable 40
Identify signer, failure to..............67
Illegal and improper acts 64–68
Immigration 58
    Documents.................................58
    Naturalization certificates..........58
Impartiality of notary....................50
Incomplete documents......**13**, 22, 50
                    65
Insurance, errors and omissions.....6
Interest
    Beneficial **11**
    Disqualifying............................ **11**
    Financial................................... **11**
Inventorying a safe-deposit box... 21
                    30–31, 99
    Certificate for 30–31, 99
    Journal signature 30
    Procedure............................ 30, **99**
    Purpose **30–31**

J
Journal of notarial acts 5–6, 14
                    43–45
    Complete first 14
    Copies of notarial records.. 29, 44
    Credible identifying witness,
        entry for...........................42–43
    Entries recommended ...14, 43–44
    Never surrender..................44–45
    Person directing Notary to sign,
        entry for..............................55
    Recommended..........................43
    Sequential record......................43

Page numbers listed in **bold** indicate where the most complete information on a subject can be found. *Italics* indicate the pages where the statutes pertaining to a subject are located.

Signature by mark, entry for.....52
Jurat.. 21, *85*
   Affidavit of proof, for 37
   Affirmation for 32
   Certificate for 31, *85*
   Certificate of proof, for 37
   Fee...49
   Identification...................... 31, *86*
   Oath for.......................................32
   Purpose 31
   Stamp 6
   Verification, part of...................**31**
   Wording for................................32
Jurisdiction.............................. 18, *82*

L

Law enforcement officers....... 19, *91*
Laws, Notary.............. 15, 51, 81–114
Law, unauthorized practice
   of 14–15, **52**, 66, 83
   Advice 15, **52**
   Assistance............................ 15, **52**
   Blank spaces in document. 13, **50**
   Exceptions...................................52
   Preparation of document 15
   Selection of document 15
   Selection of notarization 15
Legalization. *See* **Authentication**
Liability
   Employer, of 68, *87*
   Notary, of.......... 15, 18, 50, 68, *84*
   Surety, of............................ 18, *84*
Living wills.....................................61
Locus sigilli 45**,** 48
Loose certificates 9, 15, 45, **46–47**
   Protection for 15
L.S...45, 48

M

Mandatory Notary course....... 16, *97*
Mark, signature by..................52–54
   Certificates for......... 52–53, *89–90*
   Witnesses 52–53
Marriage
   Ceremony in Spanish 116–117
Marriages....21, **32–34**, *84*, *113–114*
   Authority to perform.. **32**, *113–114*
   Ceremony............ 32–33, *113–114*
   Certificate for 34

Fees 34, 49, *84*
   Procedure...................................32
   Relatives, performing for...........34
Mentally incapacitated signer . 12–13
   22, 65, 67, *92*
Military officer notarizations ... 59–60
   104
   Certificate 59–60, *104*
   Worldwide jurisdiction...59–60, *104*
Minors, notarizing for.............55–56
   Age of majority 55–56
   Identification........................55–56
   Include age next to
     signature..........................55–56
   Procedure.............................55–56
   Signature 55–56
Misconduct... 22–23, **64–68**, 83, *113*
   Acknowledgment in lieu of
     oath................................. 67, *84*
   Address change, failure to
     report...............................20, 64
   Advertising, false or
     misleading 57, 66, 83, *87*
   Application misstatement....17, 83
   Beneficial interest.............. 65, *93*
   Blank certificates, signing .. 66, *92*
   Bond, failure to maintain....64, 83
   Certifying copies of recordable
     documents...............................65
   Civil penalties for ... 64–68, *84–89*
   Commission name 64
   Commission suspension............64
   Complaints against Notary . 68, *83*
   Correcting certificate **47**, 67
   Criminal record......................... *82*
   Defined 64–65
   Defraud, intent to 64, 83
   Employer liability 68, *87*
   Facsimile signature, Notary...67, *92*
   False certificate 47, 66
   Falsely acting as a Notary 64
     83, *87*
   False name, signing...... **23**, 66, *87*
     92
   Fictious name, applying with ... 17
     64, *82*
   Financial interest................. 65, *93*
   Foreign-language signers ... **58**, 67
   Fraud 64–68, *83*

Identify signer, failure to 67, *86*
Incomplete document,
  notarizing 65, *93*
Insurance 6
Investigation into 68
Law, unauthorized practice of .. 15
  51–52, 66, 83, *87*
Liability for..15, 18, **51–52**, 68, 84
Maintenance of commission 64
Mentally incapacitated
  signer............. 12–13, **22**, 65, *92*
Misrepresentation 17, **67**, *82*
Name change, failure to
  report.............................. **20**, 64
Notarizing for relatives..............65
Notarizing own signature..........22
Overcharging 50, **67**, 83
Own signature, notarizing ..**22**, 65
  84
Personal appearance, failure to
  require 22, **65**, *92*
Recordable documents,
  notarizing **65**
Refusal of services............ 8–9, **51**
Relatives, notarizing for....... 11, 23
  65, *93*
Revocation of commission.. 64–67
  82
Seal, lost or damaged and not
  reported........................... 48, *85*
Seal, misusing 68, *85*
Seal, unlawful possession of..... 66
  85
Self-notarization 65
Signing false name 23, 66
Suspension of commission.. 64, *82*
Unauthorized practice of law ... 83
  98
Unlawful possession of seal 66
Vital records, notarizing 22, **65**

N

Name
  False or fictious ... 4, 17, 23, 64, 66
  82–83, 84, 92

Notary's change of.........20, 64, 83
Name, change of 87
National Notary Association.. 125–127
Naturalization certificates.............58
Notarial acts 21–38
  Acknowledgments ... 21, 23–27, *84*
  85–86, 88–89, 103
  Affirmations...... 22, **34–36**, *88–90*
  Authorized acts 21–22
  Certified copies...... 21, **28–30**, *87*
  Choosing 14, 52
  Inventorying a safe-deposit
    box.................................. 21, *99*
  Jurats 21, **31–32**, *85–86*
  Marriages.......................21, **32–34**
  Oaths..........22, **34–36**, *84, 88–90*
  Proof of execution by subscribing
    witness...........................**36–37**
  Unauthorized acts......................22
  Verifying a vehicle identification
    number 22
Notarial certificates...... 6, 14, **44–46**
  Choosing 46
  Contents 45–46
  Correcting 47
  False certificate 47
  Loose certificates 46
  Marriage 34
  Pre-signed or pre-sealed 47
  Requirement................................44
Notarial journal......................5–6, 14
Notarial records
  Copies of..............................29–30
Notarizing own signature....... 65, *84*
Notary bond.............................. 4, *95*
Notary, Florida civil-law...............19
Notary seal. *See* **Seal, notarial**
Notary's tools 5

O

Oath of office, Notary's............4, **18**
  Filing 18, *83*
  Requirement....................... 18, *82*
Oaths..........................22, **31–32**, 84
  Affidavit, for................................62

Page numbers listed in **bold** indicate where the most complete information on a subject can be found. *Italics* indicate the pages where the statutes pertaining to a subject are located.

Ceremony......................................36
Credible identifying witnesses,
   for **8, 35**
Deposition, for....................63–64
Fee.. 49, *84*
Gestures 36
Jurat, for 31
Power to administer 34–35, *84*
Purpose 34
Response required...............36, 62
Witness in court, for..................35
Wording.....................................35
Offices of Florida Notary regulating
   officials......................................117

P

Penalties. *See* **Misconduct**
Personal appearance ...11, **12**, 22, 31
   37, 46, *92*
Personal knowledge of identity......8
   12, 23, 26, 31, **38–39**, 40, 42, 43
   54, 56, *86*
Photocopies 9**,** 21, 28–30**,** *87–88*
Photograph, notarizing...................8
Practices and procedures 38–64
Prohibited acts. *See* **Misconduct**
Proof of execution by subscribing
   witness 22, **36–37**
   In lieu of acknowledgment.......36
   Not allowed in Florida 37
   Subscribing witness 36–37
Prothonotary, certificate of.
   See **Authentication**
Public records, notarizing 10

Q

Qualifications.....................**3**, 16, *82*

R

Reappointment 3, **19**, *82, 83*
Reasonable care........... 12–15, 51–52
Recordable documents,
   notarizing............................**65**, *88*
   Certified copies prohibited . 28–29
Refusal of services.............. 9–11, **51**
Relatives, notarizing for....**11**, 23, *93*
Renewal 3, **19**
Representative capacity..... 14, 24, 26
   44, *88–89*

Certificate for 24
   Short-form certificate for 26
Resignation of commission 20–21
   82–83
Responsibility of Notary..........51–52
Revocation of commission........... *82*
See **Misconduct**

S

Safe-deposit box, inventorying..... 21
   30–31, *99*
   Certificate for 30–31
   Fee...49
   Journal Signature 30
   Procedure...................................30
   Purpose 30
Satisfactory evidence *86*
Scilicet...45
SCT 45
Seal, notarial 4, 47–48, *85*
   Affixing................................ 45, *85*
   Certificates, notarial.................**45**
   Embosser................................... *85*
   Embosser seal 5
   Format 45, 48
   Information required...... 5, 45, *85*
   Inking seal 5, 45, 47, *85*
   Lost or misplaced 48, *85*
   L.S..45, 48
   No room for 9
   Placement of impression.... 48, *85*
   Required information 48, *85*
   Requirement for.................. 47, *85*
   Smears...9
   Unlawful possession of 48, **66**
   85
Self-notarization...................... 65, *84*
Self-proving wills..........................60
Short-form certificates 24–26
   106–107
Signature
   Certificate, on............................15
   Checking 13
   In presence of Notary **11**, 31
   Journal, in 30, 42
   Minor, of....................................55
   Notarizing one's own 22, 65, *84*
   Notary's 45, *84*

Notary's facsimile.......... 45, 67, *92*
Photocopied.................................9
Signature by mark **52–54**, *89–90*
   Certificates for......... 52–53, *89–90*
   Mark serves as signature......52–53
                      89
   Same as signature................52–54
   Witnesses for...................... 52**,** *89*
SS..45
Stamp
   Jurat..6
   Venue 6
Statement of particulars
   Certificate, notarial 45
Steps to Proper Notarization... 12–15
Subscribing witness. *See* **Proof of
execution**
Supplies.......................................5–6
Surety 17–18, *84*

T

Term of office, Notary's ... 18–19, *82*
Testimonium clause.......................45
Thumbprint.............................6, **44**
   Device 6
   Purpose 44
Tools, Notary 5
   Fingerprinting device 6
Translation of Notary Public 58

U

Unauthorized acts..........................22
   Blank certificates 22
   Certified copies of vital or public
      records 22
   Mentally incapacitated signer,
      notarizing for **22**
   Notarizing for relatives..............23
   Notarizing incomplete
      documents..............................22
   Notarizing one's own
      signature................................22
   Notarizing without
      appearance.............................22
   Notary named in document......22

Proofs of execution by
   subscribing witness................22
   Signing false names...................23
Unauthorized practice of
   law..........14–15, 52, 57, 66, 83, *98*
   Exceptions..................................52
Understanding, determining ... 12–13
Uniform Electronic Transactions Act
   (UETA)................................ *97–99*
Uniform Real Property Electronic
   Recording Act (URPERA) ... *97–99*
U.S. Code 59
U.S.C. 936......................................59
U.S.C. 1044a..................................59

V

Venue **45**, *106*
   Stamp 6
Verifying a vehicle identification
   number.................. 22, **37–38**, *98*
   Fees 49
   Purpose **37**
Verification form 37–38
Vital records, notarizing...........10, 22
                  28–29, **65**, *88*

W

Willingness, determining......... 12–13
Wills......................**60–61**, *111–112*
   Advice, do not offer 7–8, **60**
   Authority to notarize 60
   Certificate for 60
   Living wills...............................61
   Self-proving..............60, *111–112*
Witnesses 7, 26, 30, 43–44, 50–56
             61, *105–106*, *108–110*
   Absentee ballot, for...... 50, *84–85*
   Credible identifying....8, 26**,** 35–36
      38–43, **40–43**, 54, 56, 60–61, *86*
   Signature by mark, for ..52–54, *90*
   Subscribing 22, 34, 36–37, *103*
                         106
   Testifying in court case 35, 55
   When person cannot sign....54–55
                    89–91

Page numbers listed in **bold** indicate where the most complete information on a subject can be found. *Italics* indicate the pages where the statutes pertaining to a subject are located.

Wills, for......................................61
Witness in court, oath or affirmation
   for...35
Witness jurat. *See* **Proof of
execution by subscribing
witness**

BEFORE YOU NOTARIZE — BE PREPARED WITH THE NNA.

If you are thinking of becoming a Notary or are an experienced Notary, the National Notary Association is your best resource for training and support! They are committed to you...
— **Nancy R., Bakersfield, CA**

Thorough knowledge of your state's statutes and standard procedures is essential to performing error-free signings. Whether you need state-required training or desire to improve your skills and proficiency, the NNA has the training you want to suit your needs.

- Online Courses
- Self-Study Books
- Annual Conference
- Webinars

THE LEADER IN NOTARY TRAINING SINCE 1957.

Learn more at www.NationalNotary.org/Training

THERE FOR YOU DURING YOUR NOTARY COMMISSION.

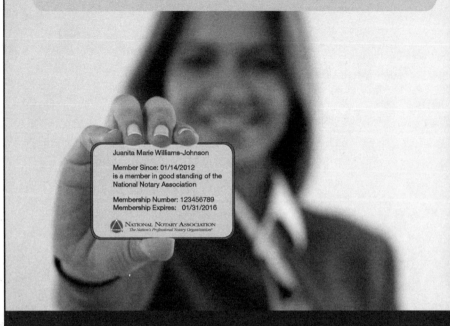

Juanita Marie Williams-Johnson

Member Since: 01/14/2012
is a member in good standing of the
National Notary Association

Membership Number: 123456789
Membership Expires: 01/31/2016

NATIONAL NOTARY ASSOCIATION
The Nation's Professional Notary Organization®

Becoming a member of the NNA means you've chosen a path to enhance your career and better serve your customers. You have separated yourself as a Notary committed to advanced education, the highest levels of professional standards and superior customer service. Valuable benefits, support and networking opportunities are yours when you join today.

- **Unlimited access to our toll-free Notary Hotline** — there for you when you need a tough notarization question answered quickly.

- **Weekly newsletters and bi-monthly magazine** featuring the latest industry updates.

- **Exclusive member-only discount pricing** on education, supplies, bonds, and E&O insurance.

- **Personal and professional growth opportunities** through high-quality education and training resources.

Join today by visiting
www.NationalNotary.org/Join

PROTECTION NOW AND AFTER YOUR COMMISSION ENDS.

If an unintentional mistake is made, or a false claim is filed against you, it could cost you thousands of dollars to defend yourself in a lawsuit. With Errors & Omissions Insurance from the NNA, you don't have to worry. Various limits of liability are available to meet your individual needs, and your policy:

- Covers the claim, legal defense fees, and court costs up to your policy's limit
- Doesn't require repayment of claims by the Notary
- Doesn't require a deductible payment

Purchase peace of mind now by visiting www.NationalNotary.org/Insurance or calling 1-888-896-6827

Source Code
A46151